THE 7 CONTIN

NORTH AMERICA

CONTENTS

Downloadable Maps

Ten maps used in this book are available for download on our Web site, as well as two color maps: one projection map of the world and one political map of North America.

How to Download:

1. Go to www.evan-moor.com/resources.
2. Enter your e-mail address and the resource code for this product—EMC3731.
3. You will receive an e-mail with a link to the downloadable maps.

What's in This Book

▶ **5 sections** of reproducible information and activity pages centered on five main topics: North America in the World, Political Divisions, Physical Features, Valuable Resources, and Culture.

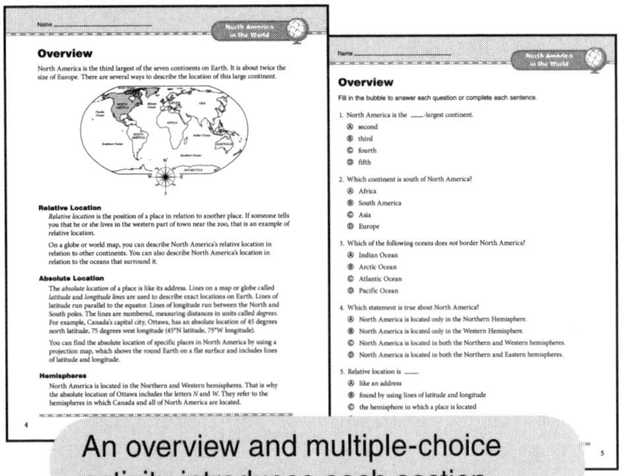

An overview and multiple-choice activity introduces each section.

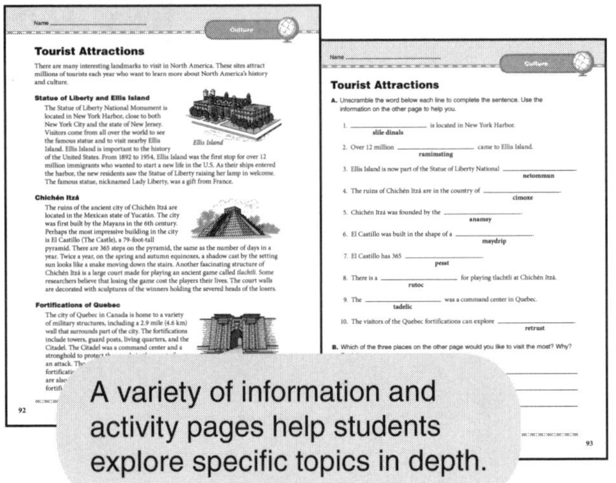

A variety of information and activity pages help students explore specific topics in depth.

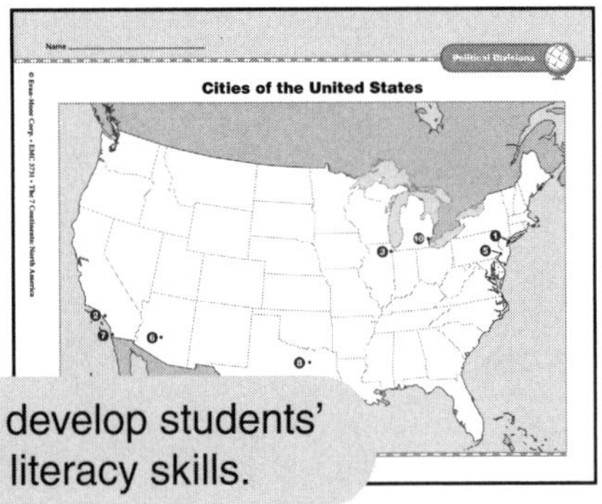

Maps develop students' visual literacy skills.

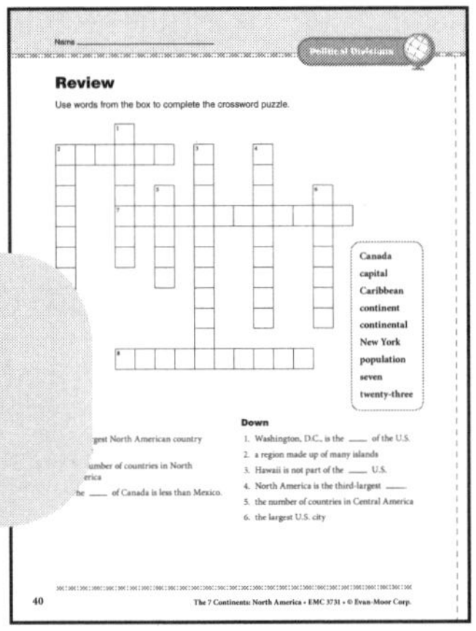

A crossword puzzle at the end of each section provides a fun review activity.

▶ **1 section** of assessment activities

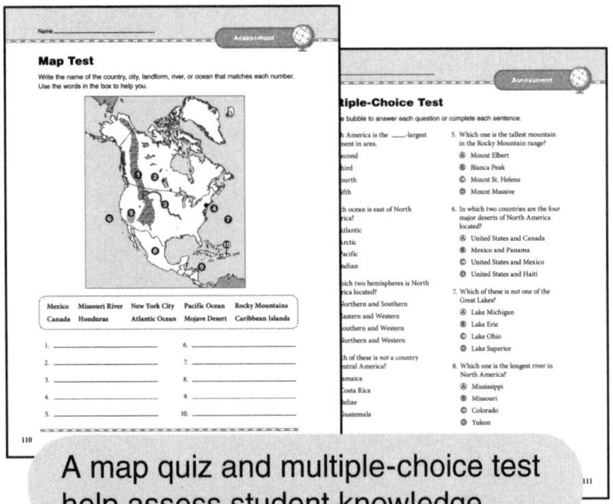

A map quiz and multiple-choice test help assess student knowledge.

▶ **1 section** of open-ended note takers

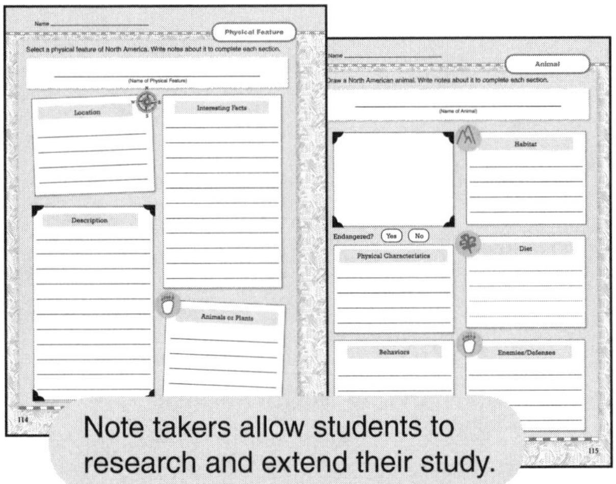

Note takers allow students to research and extend their study.

SECTION 1

North America in the World

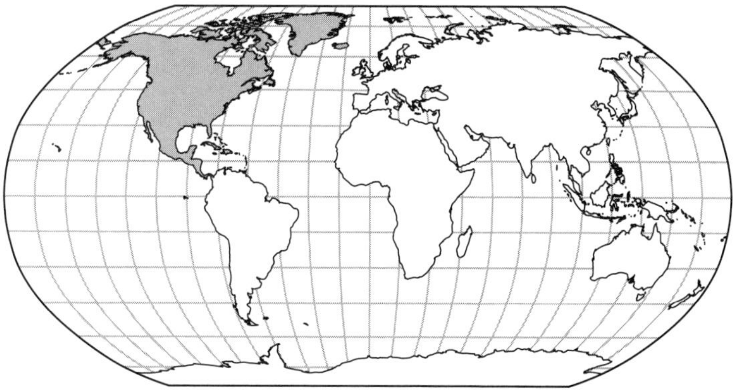

This section introduces students to the location of North America in the world. Students learn about the difference between relative and absolute location, as well as the hemispheres in which North America lies. Students also practice using lines of latitude and longitude to find places on a map.

Each skill in this section is based on the following National Geography Standards:

Essential Element 1: The World in Spatial Terms

Standard 1: How to use maps and other geographic representations, tools, and technologies to acquire, process, and report information from a spatial perspective

CONTENTS

Overview

North America is the third largest of the seven continents on Earth. It is about twice the size of Europe. There are several ways to describe the location of this large continent.

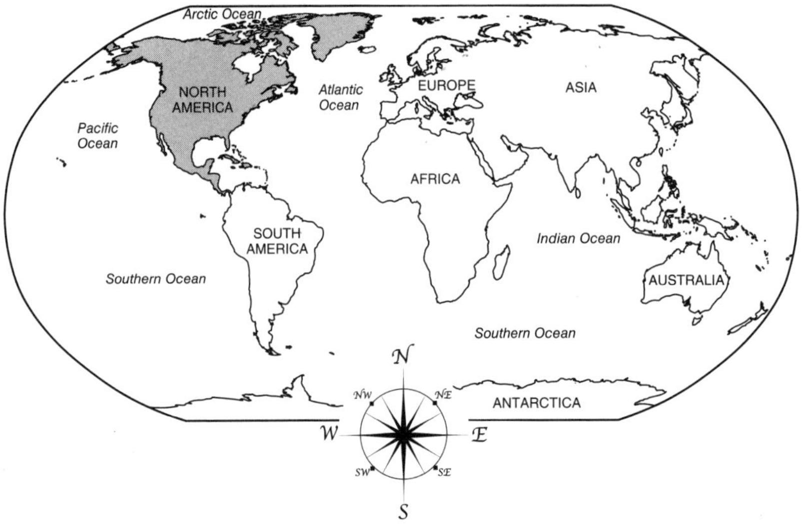

Relative Location

Relative location is the position of a place in relation to another place. If someone tells you that he or she lives in the western part of town near the zoo, that is an example of relative location.

On a globe or world map, you can describe North America's relative location in relation to other continents. You can also describe North America's location in relation to the oceans that surround it.

Absolute Location

The *absolute location* of a place is like its address. Lines on a map or globe called *latitude* and *longitude lines* are used to describe exact locations on Earth. Lines of latitude run parallel to the equator. Lines of longitude run between the North and South poles. The lines are numbered, measuring distances in units called *degrees.* For example, Canada's capital city, Ottawa, has an absolute location of 45 degrees north latitude, 75 degrees west longitude (45°N latitude, 75°W longitude).

You can find the absolute location of specific places in North America by using a projection map, which shows the round Earth on a flat surface and includes lines of latitude and longitude.

Hemispheres

North America is located in the Northern and Western hemispheres. That is why the absolute location of Ottawa includes the letters *N* and *W.* They refer to the hemispheres in which Canada and all of North America are located.

Overview

Fill in the bubble to answer each question or complete each sentence.

1. North America is the ____-largest continent.
   - Ⓐ second
   - Ⓑ third
   - Ⓒ fourth
   - Ⓓ fifth

2. Which continent is south of North America?
   - Ⓐ Africa
   - Ⓑ South America
   - Ⓒ Asia
   - Ⓓ Europe

3. Which of the following oceans does *not* border North America?
   - Ⓐ Indian Ocean
   - Ⓑ Arctic Ocean
   - Ⓒ Atlantic Ocean
   - Ⓓ Pacific Ocean

4. Which statement is true about North America?
   - Ⓐ North America is located only in the Northern Hemisphere.
   - Ⓑ North America is located only in the Western Hemisphere.
   - Ⓒ North America is located in both the Northern and Western hemispheres.
   - Ⓓ North America is located in both the Northern and Eastern hemispheres.

5. Relative location is ____.
   - Ⓐ like an address
   - Ⓑ found by using lines of latitude and longitude
   - Ⓒ the hemisphere in which a place is located
   - Ⓓ the location of a place compared to another place

North America's Relative Location

Relative location is the position of a place in relation to another place. How would you describe where North America is located in the world using relative location?

Look at the world map on the other page. One way to describe North America's relative location is to name the other continents that border it. For example, North America is west of Europe and north of South America.

Another way to describe the relative location of North America is to name the oceans that surround the continent. For example, the Atlantic Ocean is east of North America, and the Pacific Ocean is west of it.

A. Use the map on the other page to complete the paragraph about the relative location of North America.

North America is the third-largest continent in the world. It is located directly west of the continent of ____________________. South America is to the ____________________ of North America. To the north is the cold ____________________ Ocean, while the Atlantic Ocean is ____________________ of North America. The ____________________ Ocean borders the continent to the west.

B. Follow the directions to color the map on the other page.

1. Color the continent south of North America orange.
2. Use blue to circle the name of the ocean that is east of North America.
3. Draw a lion on the continent that is across the ocean from and southeast of North America.
4. A narrow strip of land connects North America to South America. Circle it with yellow.
5. Greenland is a large North American island to the northeast of the main part of the continent. Color Greenland green.

Name ______________________

North America's Relative Location

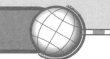

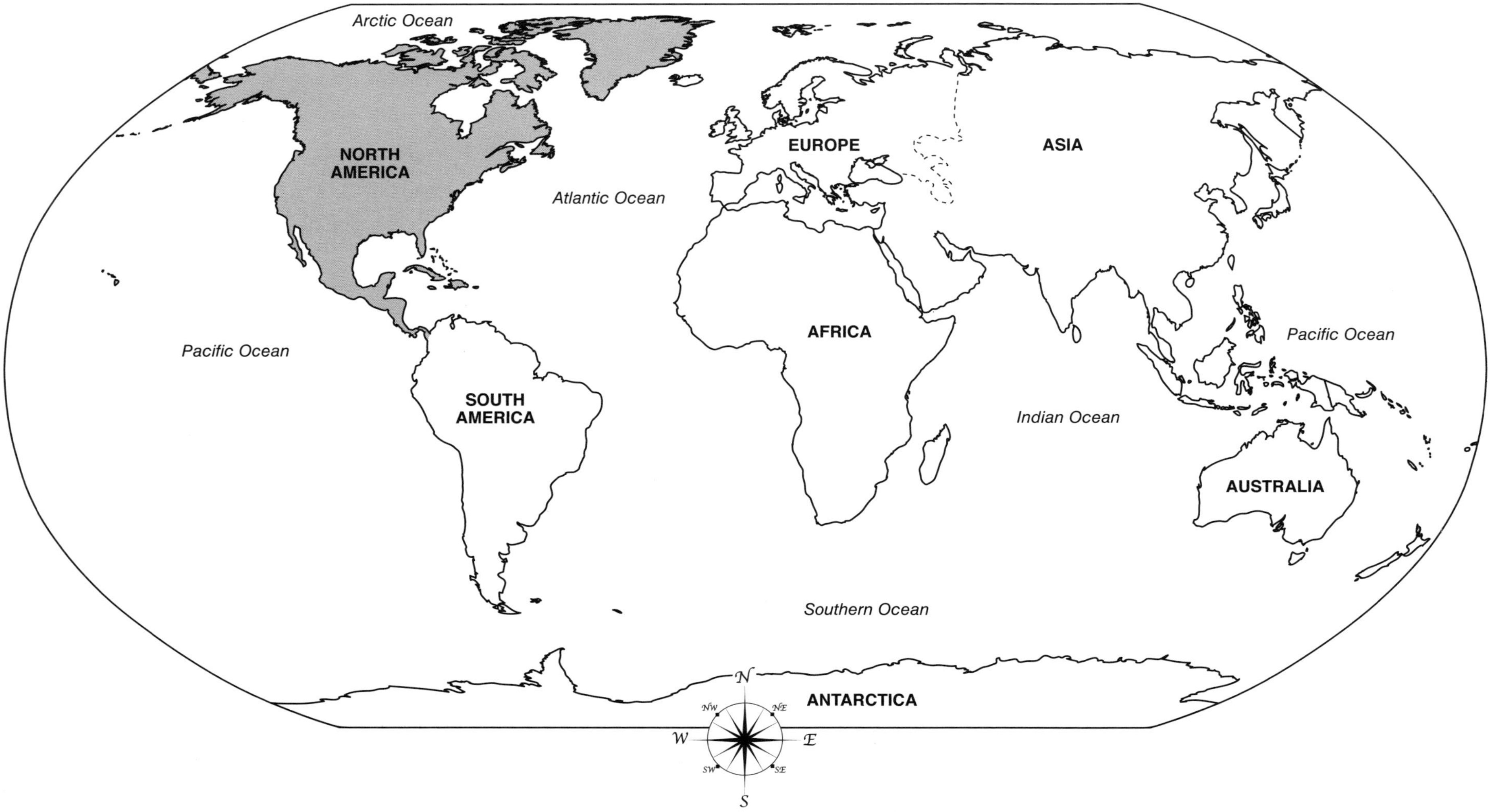

Name ________________________

North America's Hemispheres

On a globe, Earth is divided into four hemispheres by a horizontal line called the *equator* and by vertical lines that run from the North Pole to the South Pole. The hemispheres are the Northern, Southern, Western, and Eastern. North America is in the Northern Hemisphere because it is north of the equator. North America is also located in the Western Hemisphere.

Northern and Southern Hemispheres

A globe shows an imaginary horizontal line that runs around the center of Earth. This line is called the equator. The equator divides Earth into the Northern and Southern hemispheres.

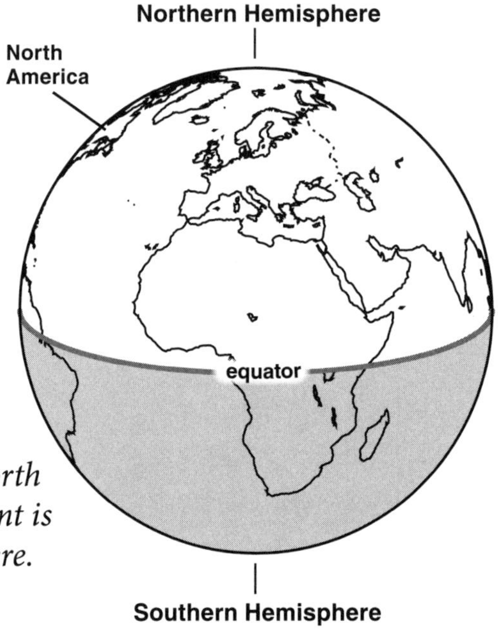

Since North America is north of the equator, the continent is in the Northern Hemisphere.

Western and Eastern Hemispheres

A globe also shows imaginary vertical lines that run from the North Pole, the northernmost point on Earth, to the South Pole. One of these lines is called the *prime meridian.* This line, along with its twin line on the opposite side of the globe, creates the Western and Eastern hemispheres.

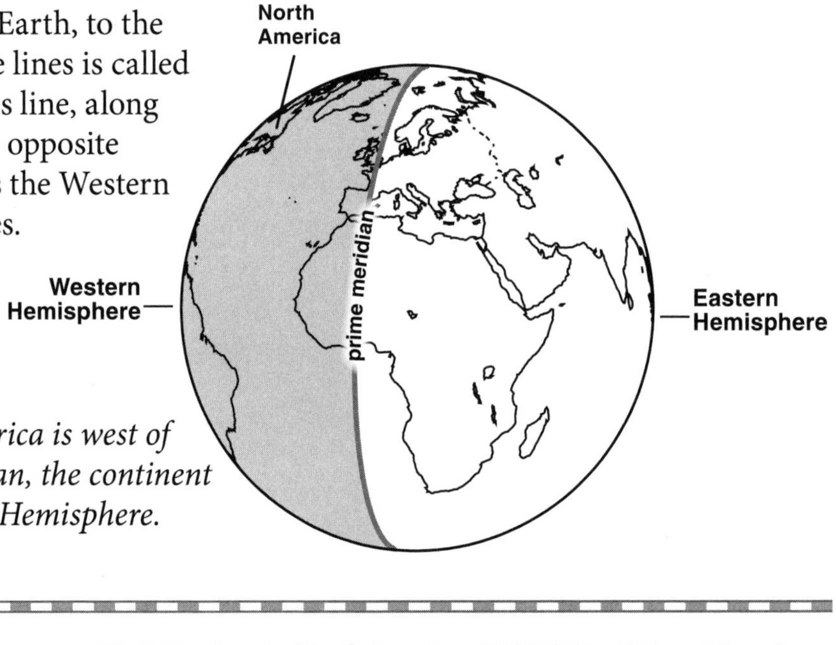

Since North America is west of the prime meridian, the continent is in the Western Hemisphere.

North America's Hemispheres

A. Write the letter of the definition that matches each term. Use the information and pictures of the globes on the other page to help you.

____ 1. North America

____ 2. continent

____ 3. globe

____ 4. equator

____ 5. Western Hemisphere

____ 6. hemisphere

____ 7. North Pole

____ 8. Northern Hemisphere

____ 9. prime meridian

a. an imaginary line that runs from the North Pole to the South Pole

b. half of Earth

c. the continent that is in both the Northern and Western hemispheres

d. the hemisphere that is west of the prime meridian

e. an imaginary line that divides Earth into the Northern and Southern hemispheres

f. one of the seven large landmasses of Earth

g. the northernmost point on Earth

h. a round model of Earth

i. the hemisphere that is north of the equator

B. Label the parts of the globe. Use the letters next to the terms in the box.

A. Western Hemisphere

B. North America

C. Northern Hemisphere

D. equator

E. prime meridian

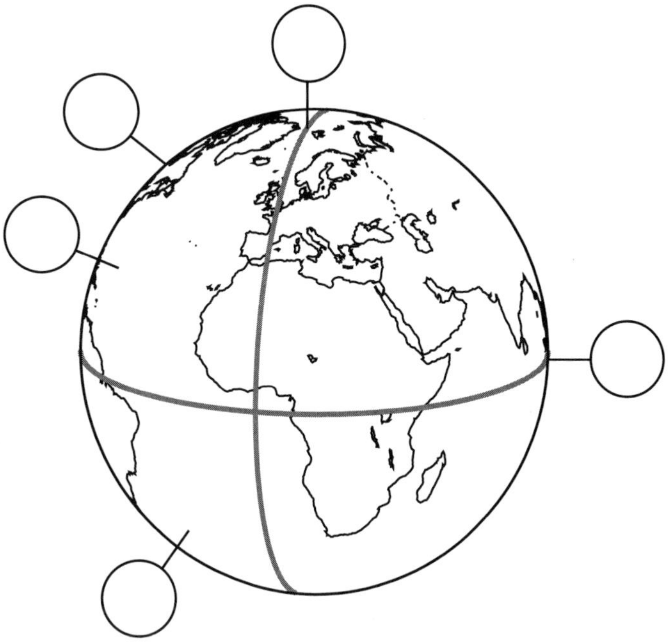

North America's Absolute Location

Many globes contain lines that make it easier to find specific places on Earth. Lines of latitude measure the distance north and south of the equator. Lines of longitude measure the distance west and east of the prime meridian. You can use lines of latitude and longitude to find the absolute location of North America on a globe.

Latitude

The equator is found at the absolute location of 0° (zero degrees) latitude. Other lines of latitude run parallel to the equator and are labeled with an *N* or *S*, depending on whether they are north or south of the equator. Latitude lines are also called *parallels*.

On the picture of the globe, notice the lines of latitude. Look for the continent of North America. Since the entire continent is north of the equator, all the latitude lines used to find North America's absolute location are labeled in *degrees north*, or °*N*.

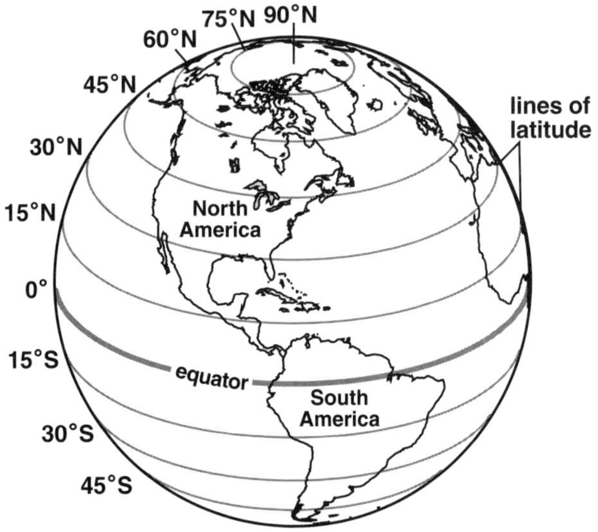

Lines of Latitude (Parallels)

Longitude

The prime meridian runs from the North Pole to the South Pole at 0° (zero degrees) longitude. Other lines of longitude run north and south, too, and are labeled with an *E* or *W*, depending on whether they are east or west of the prime meridian. Longitude lines are also called *meridians*.

On the picture of the globe, notice the lines of longitude. Look for the continent of North America. Since the entire continent is west of the prime meridian, all of the longitude lines used to find North America's absolute location are labeled in *degrees west*, or °*W*.

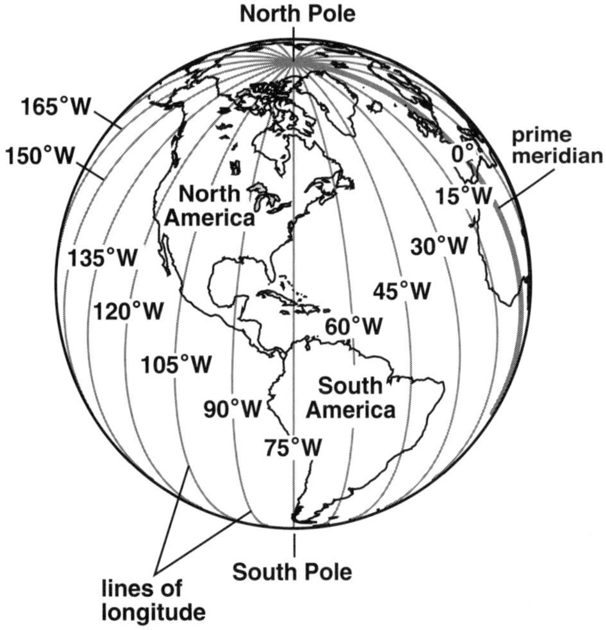

Lines of Longitude (Meridians)

North America's Absolute Location

To find the absolute location of a place, read the latitude line first and then read the longitude line. For example, the latitude 25°N runs through the southern part of the United States. The longitude 80°W runs through the eastern part of the United States. So the absolute location of the southeastern United States, or the state of Florida, is 25°N latitude, 80°W longitude.

A. Circle the answer to each question. Use the pictures of the globes and information on the other page to help you.

1. Which line is at zero degrees latitude?	**equator**	**prime meridian**
2. Which line runs north and south?	**equator**	**prime meridian**
3. Which line of longitude runs through North America?	**100°E**	**100°W**
4. Where is the North Pole located?	**90°S**	**90°N**
5. Which lines run parallel to the equator?	**latitude lines**	**longitude lines**
6. How many degrees are between each line of latitude and longitude on the globes?	**10 degrees**	**15 degrees**
7. What is another name for *lines of latitude*?	**meridians**	**parallels**
8. Which line of latitude is closer to the equator?	**40°N**	**60°S**
9. Which line of longitude is farther west?	**150°W**	**120°W**

B. Using the information on the other page, explain why all places in North America have absolute locations that are labeled in degrees north and west.

____

____

Using a Projection Map

How do you draw a picture of a round object, like Earth, on a flat piece of paper? In order to show all of Earth's continents and oceans in one view, mapmakers use a system called *projection*. Mapping the round Earth on a flat surface causes some areas to look bigger than they really are. For example, land near the poles gets stretched out when flattened. That's why Greenland and Antarctica look so big on some maps.

A projection map of the world shows all the lines of latitude and longitude on Earth. Study the projection map on the other page. Notice the lines of latitude and longitude. You can use these lines to find the absolute location of a specific place in North America. For example, the label *North America* is located at 45°N latitude, 105°W longitude.

Read each statement. Circle **yes** if it is true or **no** if it is false. Use the map on the other page to help you.

1. North America is located on the prime meridian. **Yes** **No**
2. North America is located north of the equator. **Yes** **No**
3. All of the southern part of North America is between the latitudes of 15°S and 30°S. **Yes** **No**
4. North America is the only continent west of the prime meridian. **Yes** **No**
5. North America shares some of the same north latitude lines with Asia. **Yes** **No**
6. North America shares some of the same west longitude lines with Europe. **Yes** **No**
7. The longitude line 60°E runs through North America and South America. **Yes** **No**
8. The latitude line 45°N runs through North America, Europe, and Asia. **Yes** **No**
9. The latitude line 75°N runs through North America and the Arctic Ocean. **Yes** **No**
10. The latitude line 60°S does not run through any continent. **Yes** **No**

Name ____________________

Using a Projection Map

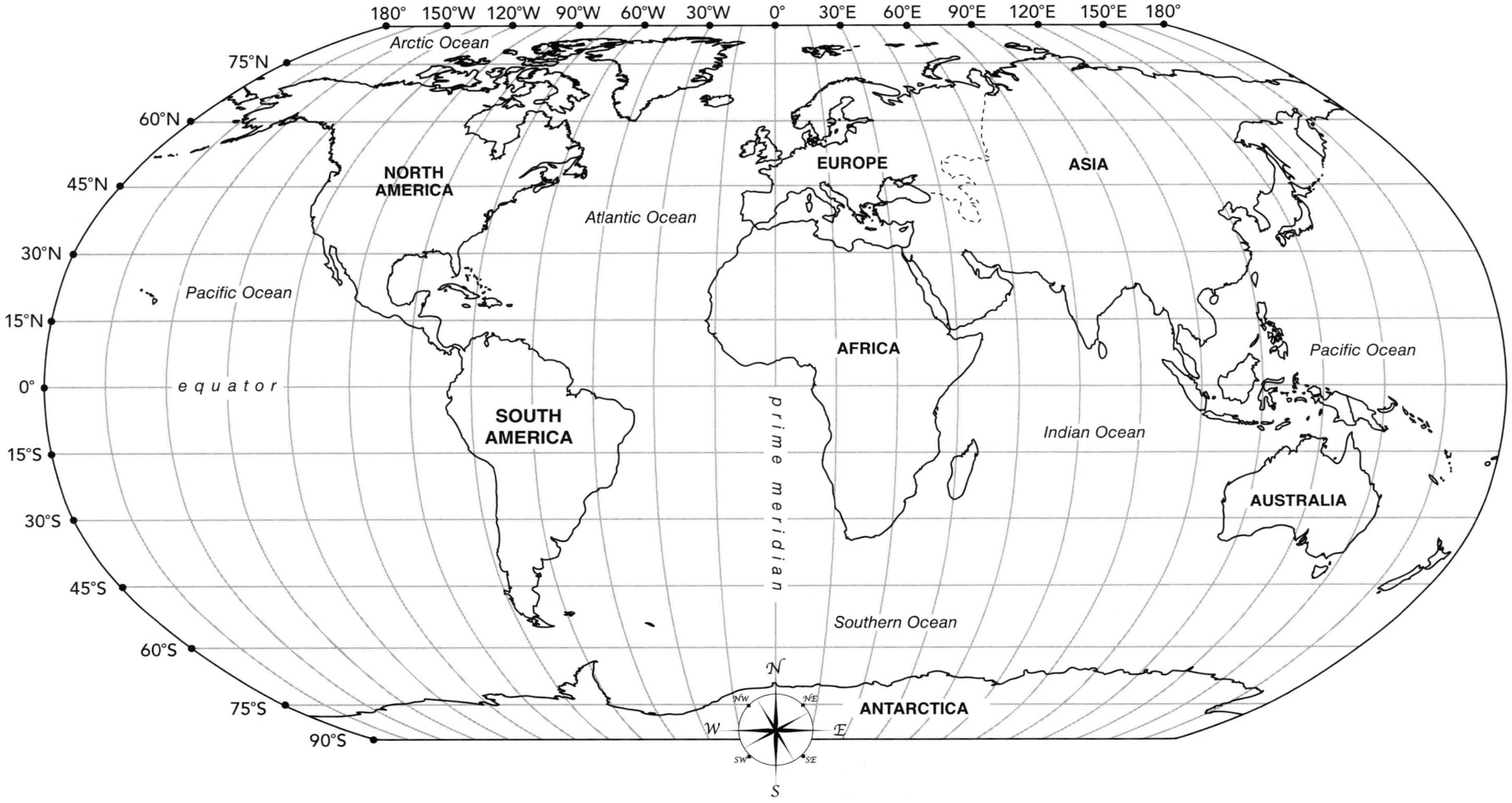

Review

Use words from the box to complete the crossword puzzle.

- Atlantic
- equator
- Europe
- Hemisphere
- Pacific
- projection
- relative
- third

Across

2. A ____ map shows the round Earth on a flat surface.
3. The Arctic, Atlantic, and ____ oceans border North America.
5. North America is located in the Northern ____.
7. North America is the ____-largest continent in the world.
8. If you go east of North America, you will find the continent of ____.

Down

1. The ____ Ocean is east of North America.
4. The ____ location is a description of a place using the relation of one place to another.
6. The ____ is the imaginary line that divides the Northern and Southern hemispheres.

SECTION 2

Political Divisions of North America

This section introduces students to the five regions and 23 countries of North America. Students learn how each region is unique and study information about the largest countries in size and population. Students also learn that the population of North America varies significantly by region.

Each skill in this section is based on the following National Geography Standards:

Essential Element 2: Places and Regions

Standard 5: People create regions to interpret Earth's complexity

Essential Element 4: Human Systems

Standard 9: The characteristics, distribution, and migration of human populations on Earth's surface

CONTENTS

Overview

North America is the third-largest continent in size and the fourth largest in population.

- North America covers about 16% of the world's landmass.
- North America has about 8% of the world's people—530 million.

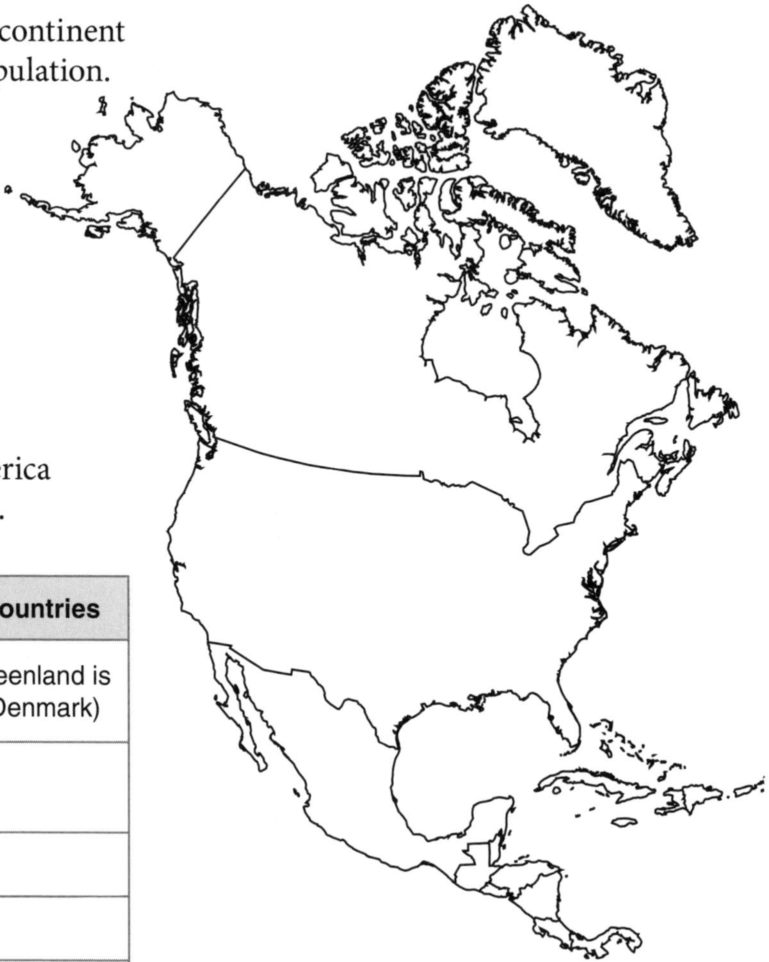

The Five Regions

The 23 countries in North America can be divided into five regions.

Region	Number of Countries
Canada and Greenland	1 country (Greenland is a territory of Denmark)
United States of America	1 country
Mexico	1 country
Central America	7 countries
Caribbean	13 countries and many small island territories

Where People Live

Over half the people who live in North America live in the United States. The eastern half of the U.S. is more densely populated than the west, especially near the northern Atlantic coast and the Great Lakes. The largest city in the United States is New York City, which is part of New York State. There are more than 8 million people in New York City.

Mexico also has a large population, with most people living in urban areas. Mexico City is the country's largest city, with a population of over 8 million people. Very few people live in Greenland and in the colder areas of Canada.

Overview

Fill in the bubble to complete each sentence.

1. North America is the ____-largest continent in size.
   - Ⓐ second
   - Ⓑ third
   - Ⓒ fourth
   - Ⓓ fifth

2. There are ____ countries in North America.
   - Ⓐ 5
   - Ⓑ 13
   - Ⓒ 23
   - Ⓓ 50

3. Over half the people in North America live in ____.
   - Ⓐ the United States
   - Ⓑ Canada
   - Ⓒ Mexico
   - Ⓓ Central America

4. Most people in Mexico live ____.
   - Ⓐ in the country
   - Ⓑ in urban areas
   - Ⓒ by the beach
   - Ⓓ in Mexico City

5. The two largest cities in North America are ____.
   - Ⓐ New York and Los Angeles
   - Ⓑ New York and Toronto
   - Ⓒ Mexico City and Los Angeles
   - Ⓓ Mexico City and New York

Population of North America

Between 1950 and 2010, the world population nearly tripled to almost 7 billion. That number is expected to increase to 9 billion by 2050. While the population of North America is also growing, the rate of growth is slower than that of the world. In 1950, there were about 220 million people living in North America. The population is expected to be about 742 million by 2050.

North America's Population: 1950–2050

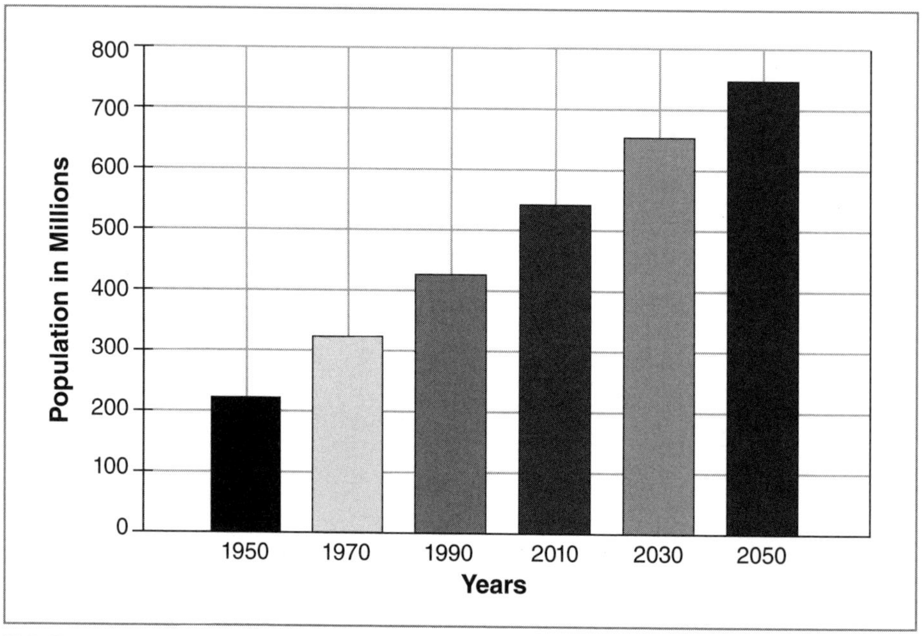

U.S. Bureau of the Census, International Data Base

A. Write two questions that can be answered by using the information on the graph. Then write the answers.

1. ____

____

____

2. ____

____

____

Population of North America

B. Circle the answer that completes each sentence. Use the information on the other page to help you.

1. The population of the world has nearly ____ since 1950.

   doubled **tripled** **quadrupled**

2. It is predicted that there will be about 9 billion people in the world by ____.

   2030 **2050** **2070**

3. The population of North America is growing at a ____ rate.

   steady **rapid** **record-breaking**

4. In 1950, there were about ____ million people living in North America.

   321 **458** **220**

5. In 2010, there were over ____ million people in North America.

   500 **600** **700**

6. By 2030, there will be about ____ million people in North America.

   423 **649** **742**

7. There are about ____ times as many people living in North America now as there were in 1950.

   two **three** **four**

8. There will be about 742 million people living in North America by ____.

   2030 **2050** **1960**

Name ______________________________

Countries of North America

North America is made up of 23 countries. Canada is the largest in size, while the smallest is Grenada, a tiny island nation in the Caribbean Sea. The United States of America is the second-largest country in size and includes a main landmass, known as the continental United States, as well as Alaska, Hawaii, Puerto Rico, and the U.S. Virgin Islands. Greenland is another part of North America, but it is not a country. It is an independent territory of the Kingdom of Denmark, which is located in Europe.

Region	Countries
Canada and Greenland	Canada
Caribbean	Antigua and Barbuda* Bahamas Barbados Cuba Dominica Dominican Republic Grenada Haiti Jamaica Saint Kitts and Nevis* Saint Lucia Saint Vincent and the Grenadines* Trinidad and Tobago
Central America	Belize Costa Rica El Salvador Guatemala Honduras Nicaragua Panama
Mexico	Mexico
United States	United States of America

* These countries are too small to be labeled on the map.

Find the five regions of North America on the map. Then use the chart and color key on this page to color the countries.

Color Key

Canada and Greenland: Green
Central America: Orange
Caribbean: Yellow
Mexico: Red
United States: Blue

Countries of North America

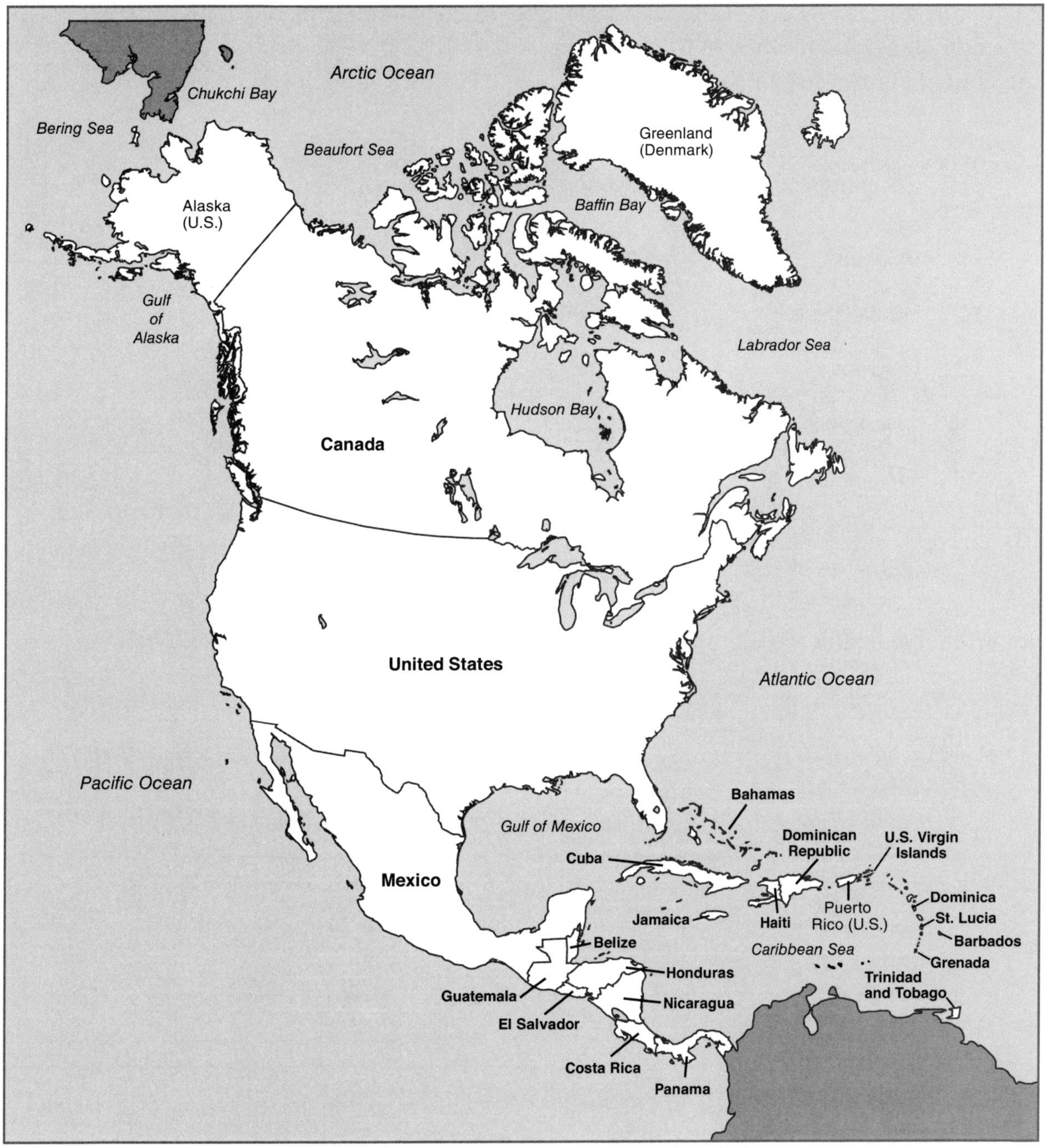

Largest Countries by Area

North America has some of the world's largest countries in terms of square miles (or kilometers). In fact, two of the four largest countries in the world—Canada and the United States—are in North America.

Rank in Size	Country	Area in Square Miles	Area in Square Kilometers
1	Canada	3,855,103	9,984,670
2	United States	3,794,100	9,826,675
3	Mexico	758,449	1,964,375
4	Nicaragua	50,336	130,370
5	Honduras	43,191	112,090

2010 CIA—The World Factbook

A. Write three statements that can be made by using information in the chart.

1. ____

____

2. ____

____

3. ____

____

B. On the map on the other page, five countries are numbered. The numbers indicate the rank of each country according to size. Color each country a different color. Then complete the map key by writing the country names in order from largest to smallest. Write the color you used for each country.

Name ____________________

Largest Countries by Area

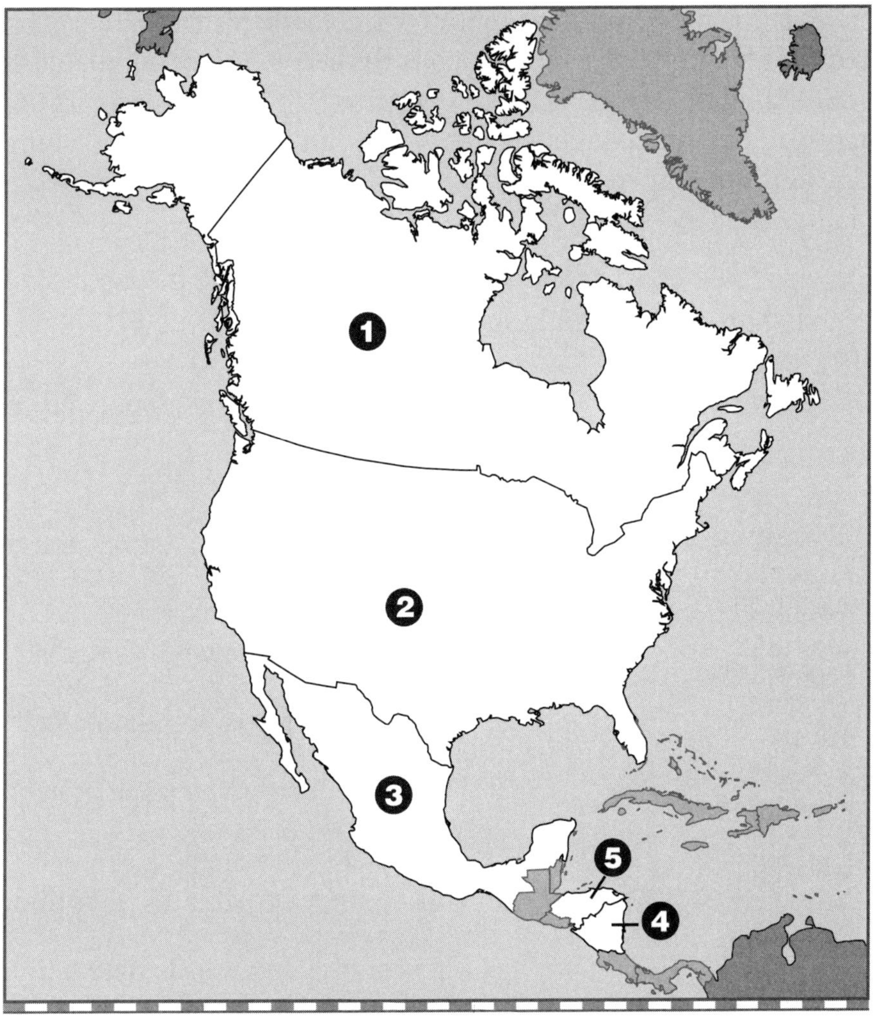

MAP KEY

The Five Largest Countries	Color
1. ____________	____________
2. ____________	____________
3. ____________	____________
4. ____________	____________
5. ____________	____________

Largest Countries by Population

The United States is the most populated country in North America. It is also the third most populated country in the world. Mexico is the second most populated country in North America. Although Canada is much bigger in size than Mexico, its population is only about one-third of Mexico's. Of the remaining ten most populated countries in North America, four are located in Central America and three are part of the Caribbean.

A. Match each clue to its country and write the letter on the line. Use the information above and the chart on the other page to help you.

_____ 1. Canada

_____ 2. Cuba

_____ 3. Dominican Republic

_____ 4. El Salvador

_____ 5. Guatemala

_____ 6. Haiti

_____ 7. Honduras

_____ 8. Mexico

_____ 9. Nicaragua

_____ 10. United States

a. This is the sixth most populated country.

b. This country has less than 6 million people.

c. This country has about 2 million more people than Cuba.

d. This country has over 300 million people.

e. This country has a population of 7,833,696.

f. This is the third most populated country in North America.

g. This country has about 11.5 million people.

h. This country has a little over 1 million more people than Nicaragua.

i. This country has 111,211,789 people.

j. This country is ranked number 7 in population.

B. Use the chart on the other page to help you answer the questions.

1. How many countries in North America have populations over 100 million? ____________

2. How many countries in North America have populations over 10 million? ____________

Largest Countries by Population

	Country	Population
1	United States	307,212,123
2	Mexico	111,211,789
3	Canada	33,487,208
4	Guatemala	13,276,517
5	Cuba	11,451,652
6	Dominican Republic	9,650,054
7	Haiti	9,035,536
8	Honduras	7,833,696
9	El Salvador	7,185,218
10	Nicaragua	5,891,199

2010 estimates, CIA—The World Factbook

C. Write three statements about the most populated countries of North America.

1. ____________________

____

2. ____________________

____

3. ____________________

____

Canada and Greenland

Although Canada is the second-largest country in the world in terms of area, it is not heavily populated. Approximately 33 million people live in Canada, making it the 36th most populated country in the world. This is because much of Canada is located in the far north where the climate is very cold, making it difficult for people to live there.

Canada is divided into 13 provinces and territories. Some of the more well-known provinces are Alberta, British Columbia, Nova Scotia, Ontario, and Quebec. The capital city of Canada is Ottawa. It is located in the province of Ontario.

Although it is located in North America, Greenland belongs to the country of Denmark in Europe. The population of Greenland is only about 57,000.

A. Read each statement. Circle **yes** if it is true or **no** if it is false. Use the information on this page and the map on the other page to help you.

1. Canada is the 34th most populated country in the world. **Yes** **No**
2. Canada's capital city is located in the province of Ontario. **Yes** **No**
3. The province of Alberta has no ocean coastline. **Yes** **No**
4. Greenland is northwest of Canada. **Yes** **No**
5. There are 14 provinces and territories in Canada. **Yes** **No**
6. Alberta, Saskatchewan, and Manitoba border the United States. **Yes** **No**
7. Canada is the largest country in the world. **Yes** **No**
8. Newfoundland and Labrador is a territory of Denmark. **Yes** **No**
9. Quebec is larger than Saskatchewan. **Yes** **No**
10. British Columbia is bordered by the Pacific Ocean. **Yes** **No**

Canada and Greenland

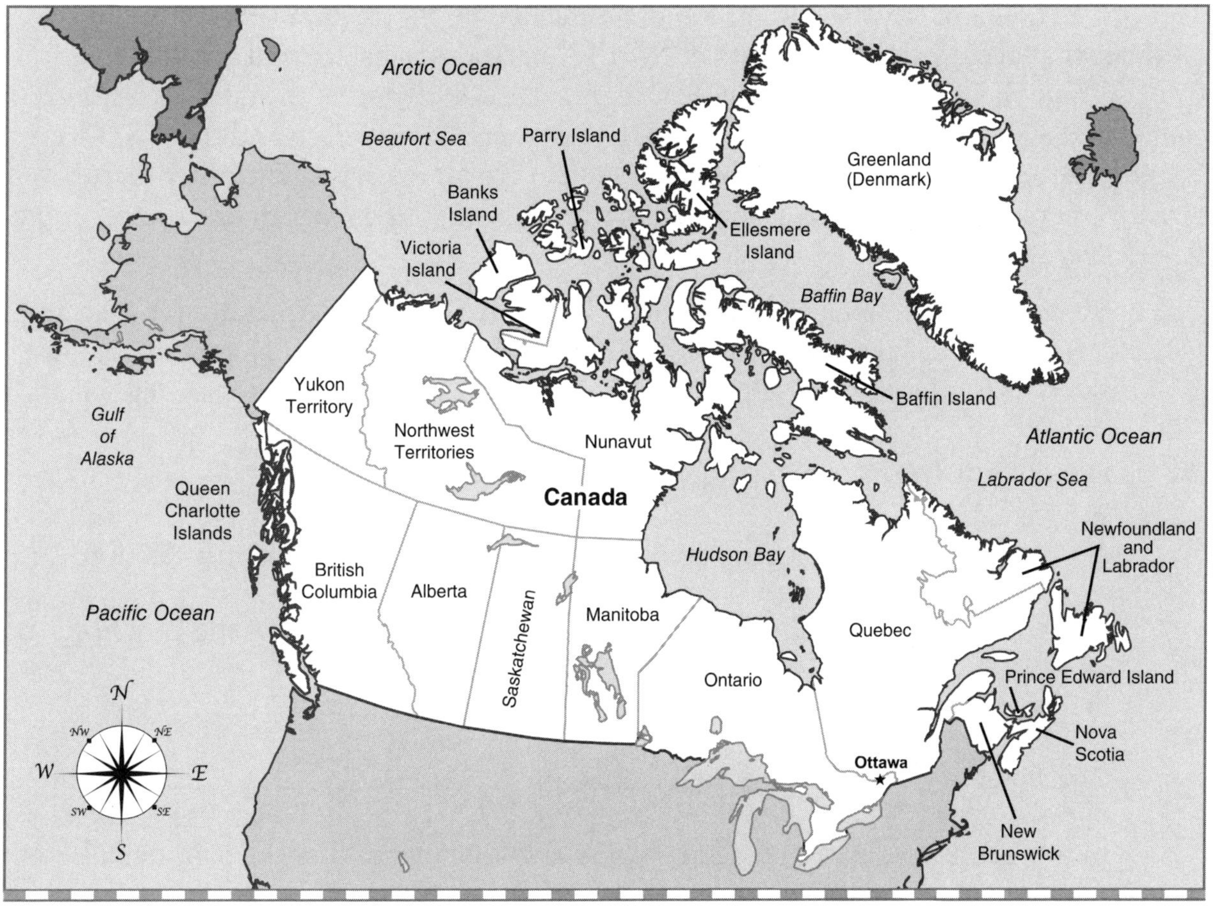

B. Write three facts about Canada and Greenland, using the information on the other page and the map on this page to help you.

1. ____

____

2. ____

____

3. ____

____

The United States and Its Territories

The United States of America is a union of 50 states. The continental U.S. is made up of 48 states that occupy the central part of North America. Alaska, located northwest of Canada, and Hawaii, in the mid-Pacific Ocean, are the 49th and 50th states. In addition, the United States possesses five territories. Two of them, Puerto Rico and the U.S. Virgin Islands, are located within the Caribbean region of North America. The other three territories are American Samoa, Guam, and the Midway Islands, which are located in the Pacific Ocean.

The 50 states can be grouped into six regions. They are the Pacific (including Alaska and Hawaii), Rocky Mountain, Southwest, North-Central, Southeast, and Northeast regions. Washington, D.C., the capital of the United States, is located in the Southeast region.

A. Use the information above to complete the paragraph.

The United States is made up of 50 states. The country can be divided into six ____________________. The ____________________ of the United States, Washington, D.C., is located in the ____________________ region. The states of ____________________ and ____________________ belong to the ____________________ region and are not a part of the continental U.S. The United States also has five ____________________, including Puerto Rico and the ____________________, which are located in North America.

B. On the map on the other page, color each of the U.S. regions a different color. Then color the key to correctly match the map.

C. Use the map on the other page to answer the questions.

1. Which region is directly west of North-Central? ____________________
2. Which region is farthest to the west? ____________________
3. Which two regions contain the Great Lakes? ____________________
4. Which two regions border the Atlantic Ocean? ____________________

The United States and Its Territories

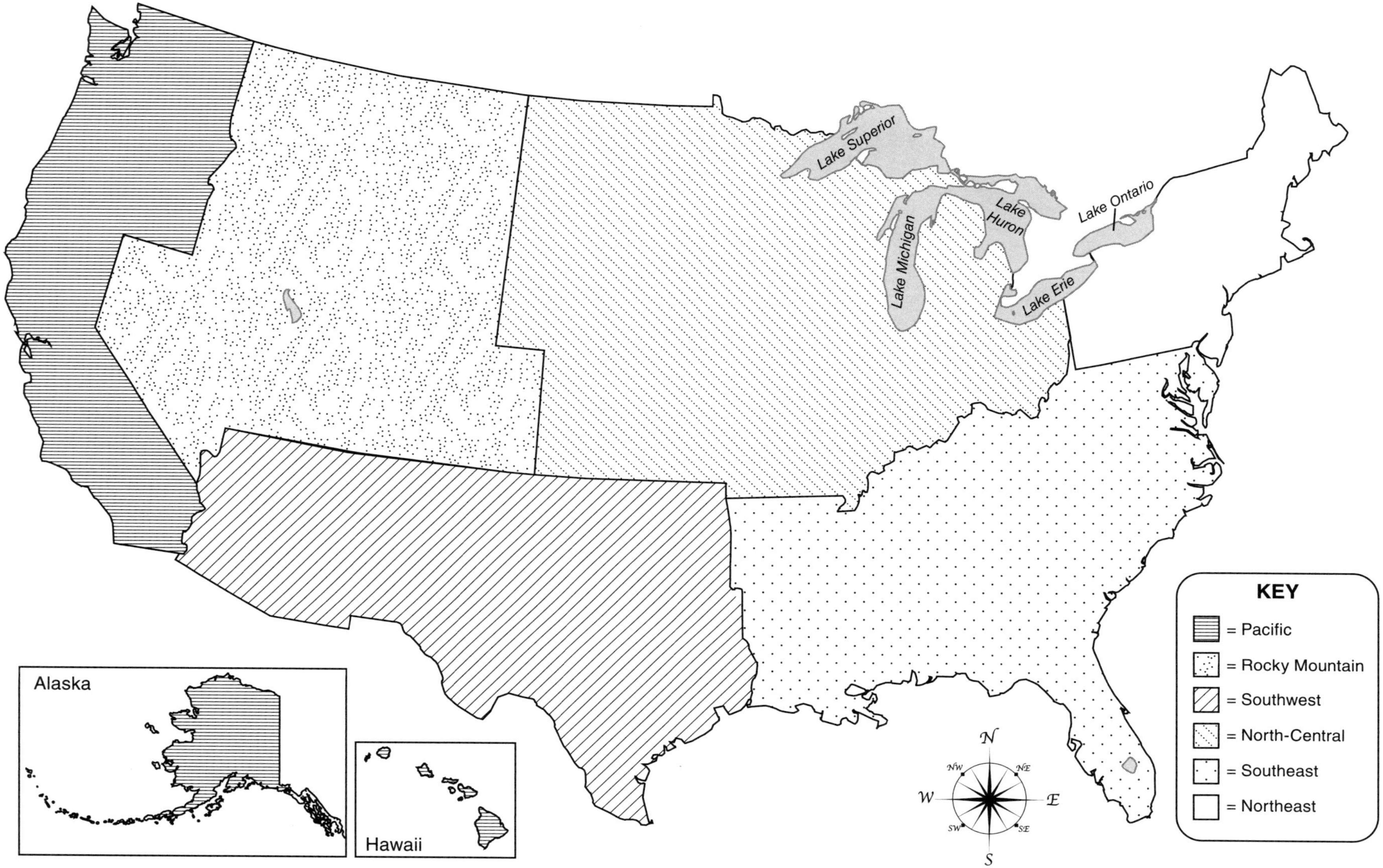

Cities of the United States

Over 300 million people live in the United States. About 80% of these people live in cities or suburbs. More people live in the eastern regions of the country than in other areas. However, more and more people are moving to the west and south. Cities in the Southwest region are starting to become more crowded.

With over 8 million people, New York City is by far the biggest city in the United States. Even Los Angeles, which is the second-biggest city, has less than half the number of people as New York. Other heavily populated cities include Chicago, Houston, Philadelphia, and Phoenix.

A. Look at the chart showing the populations of the United States' biggest cities. Then write a sentence about the information in the chart.

	City	Population
1	New York	8,008,278
2	Los Angeles	3,694,820
3	Chicago	2,896,016
4	Houston	1,593,631
5	Philadelphia	1,517,550
6	Phoenix	1,321,045
7	San Diego	1,223,400
8	Dallas	1,188,580
9	San Antonio	1,144,646
10	Detroit	951,270

____

____

B. On the map on the other page, a star marks the location of each city, along with its number according to rank in population. Write the name of each city near its star.

Name ______________________

Cities of the United States

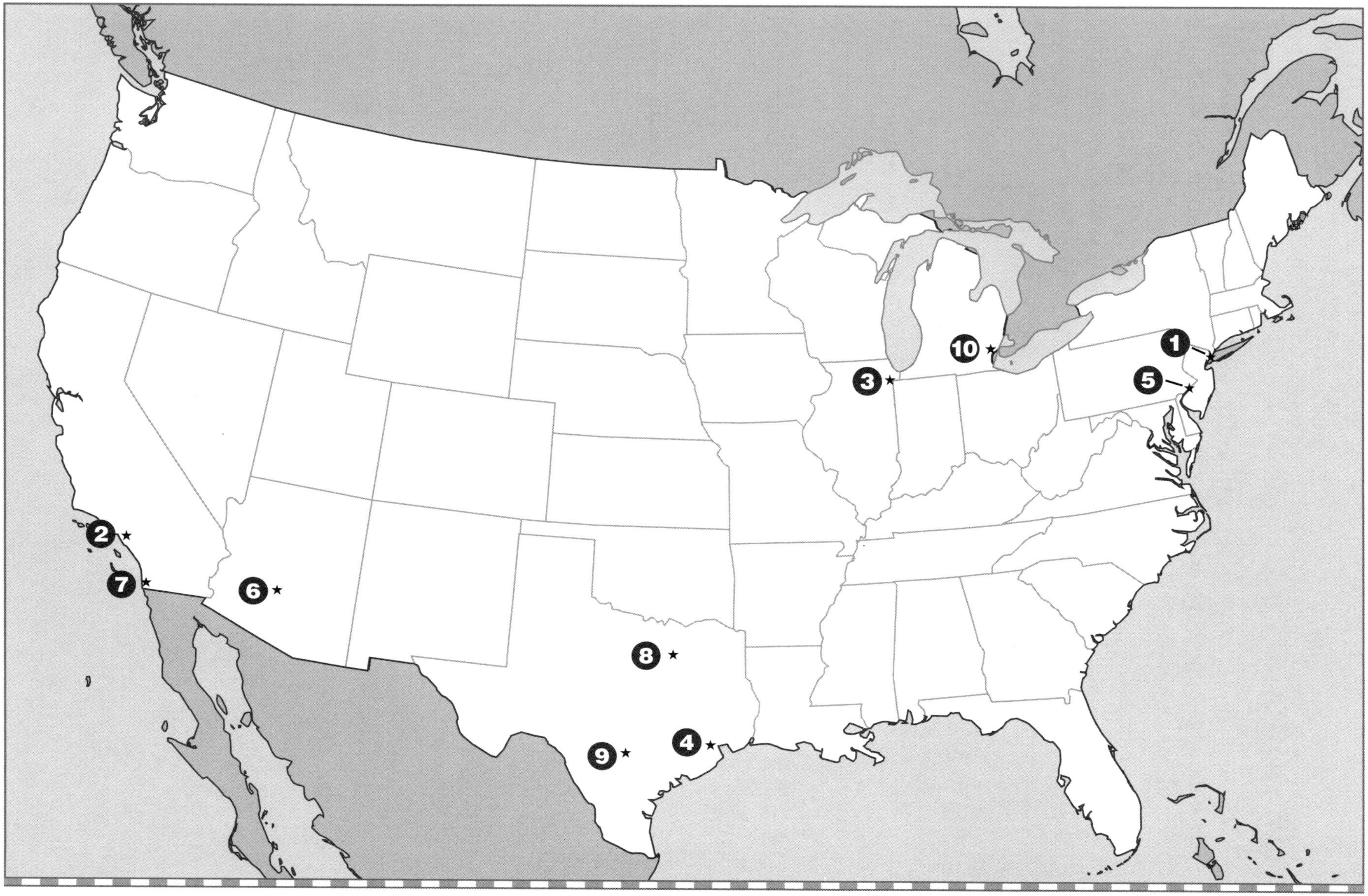

Mexico

Mexico is located just south of the United States. In terms of area, Mexico is the third-largest country in North America and the 15th largest in the world. Mexico is made up of 31 states.

Over 111 million people live in Mexico, making it the 11th most populated country in the world. Most people live in the cities. Mexico City, the capital of Mexico, is by far the largest city with more than 8 million people. Other large cities in Mexico include Guadalajara, Monterrey, Puebla, Puerto Vallarta, and Tijuana.

A. Use the information above to complete the paragraph.

Mexico is the third-largest country in ______________________ and the 15th largest in the ____________________. There are ____________________ states in Mexico. The capital city of Mexico is ______________________. It is also the largest city, with more than 8 million people.

B. Circle the answer that completes each sentence. Use the map on the other page and the information on this page to help you.

1. The state of ____ is bordered by the Pacific Ocean.

   Jalisco **Hidalgo**

2. The state of Durango is ____ of the state of Oaxaca.

   northwest **southeast**

3. The state of ____ is at the end of a peninsula.

   Chiapas **Baja California Sur**

4. ____ is one of the states that borders the United States.

   Veracruz **Coahuila**

Name ______________________

Mexico

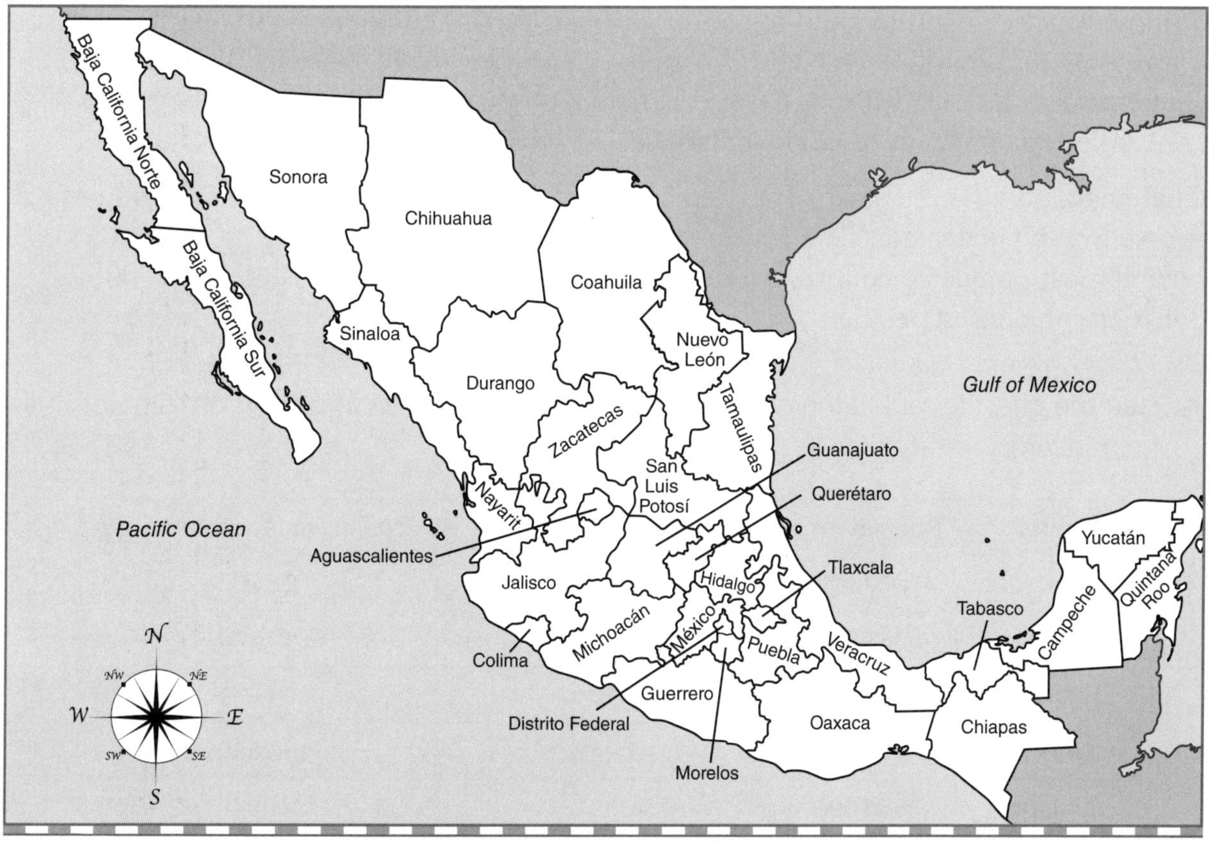

C. The United States borders Mexico to the north. Color the six Mexican states that border the U.S. Then write a caption for the map.

____

____

____

Central America

Central America is a thin band of countries located between Mexico and South America. There are seven countries in Central America. They are Belize, Costa Rica, El Salvador, Guatemala, Honduras, Nicaragua, and Panama. Of these, Nicaragua is the largest in area, followed by Honduras and Guatemala.

Guatemala is by far the most populated country in Central America. Over 13 million people live in Guatemala. That is nearly twice the number of people living in the second most populated country, Honduras. With a population of just over 300,000, Belize has the fewest people.

A. Use the chart to rank each country by population and area in order from largest to smallest.

Country	Population	Area in Square Miles	Area in Square Kilometers
Belize	307,899	8,867	22,966
Costa Rica	4,353,877	19,730	51,100
El Salvador	7,185,218	8,124	21,041
Guatemala	13,276,517	42,042	108,889
Honduras	7,833,696	43,191	111,864
Nicaragua	5,891,199	50,336	130,370
Panama	3,360,474	29,120	75,420

2010 CIA—The World Factbook

Population	Area
1. ________________	1. ________________
2. ________________	2. ________________
3. ________________	3. ________________
4. ________________	4. ________________
5. ________________	5. ________________
6. ________________	6. ________________
7. ________________	7. ________________

Central America

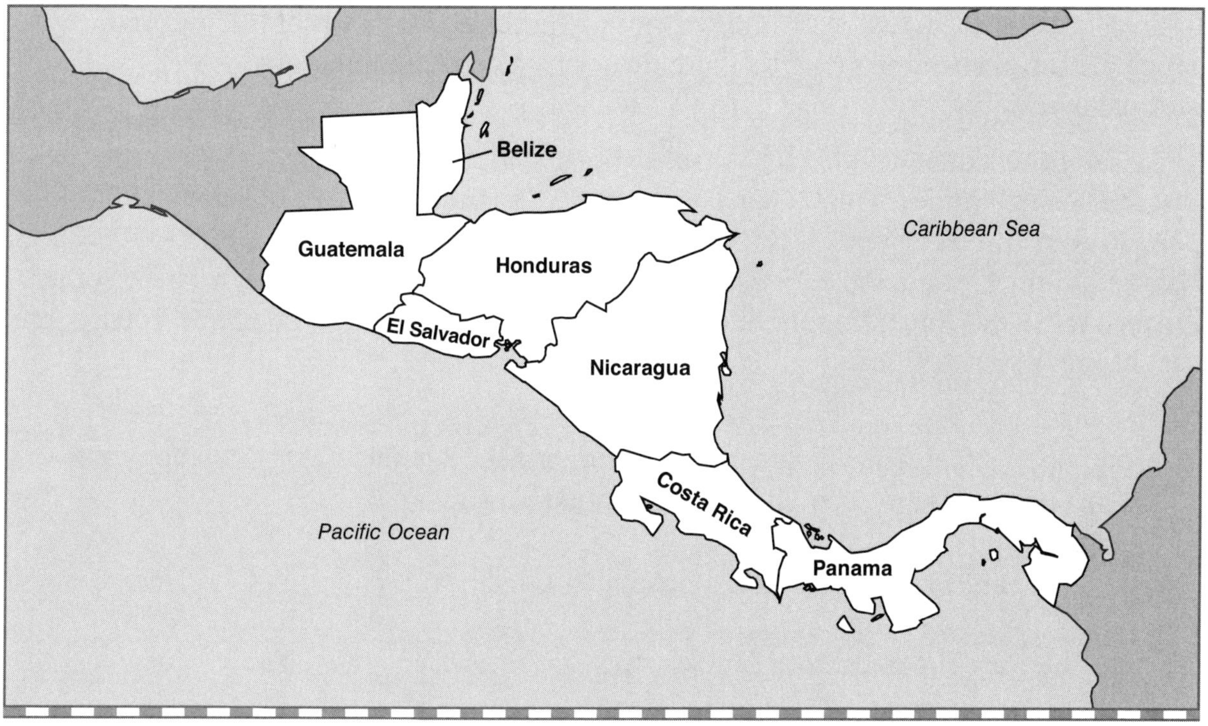

B. Color each Central American country a different color. Then write a caption for the map, using the words *area*, *largest*, and *smallest*.

____

____

____

C. Use information from the map to help you write two statements about Central America.

1. ____

____

2. ____

____

The Caribbean

In the Caribbean Sea, east of Central America, there are thousands of islands, many of which are uninhabited. Among these, there are 13 independent nations, as well as 11 territories.

The Caribbean can be divided into three regions: the Bahamas, the Greater Antilles, and the Lesser Antilles. The Bahamas is a group of islands southeast of the tip of Florida. The Greater Antilles is west of the Bahamas and includes Cuba, Jamaica, Puerto Rico, and Hispaniola, on which both Haiti and the Dominican Republic are located. All of the other Caribbean Islands, including the Virgin Islands, Barbados, and Trinidad and Tobago, are part of the Lesser Antilles.

A. Read each statement. Circle **yes** if it is true or **no** if it is false. Use the information on this page and the map on the other page to help you.

1. There are 13 independent nations in the Caribbean. **Yes** **No**
2. There are thousands of islands in the Caribbean. **Yes** **No**
3. The Bahamas are located southwest of the tip of Florida. **Yes** **No**
4. Cuba is part of the Bahamas. **Yes** **No**
5. Dominica is an island in the Lesser Antilles. **Yes** **No**
6. Haiti and the Dominican Republic are on the island of Hispaniola. **Yes** **No**
7. St. Lucia is part of the Greater Antilles. **Yes** **No**
8. Cuba is southwest of the Bahamas. **Yes** **No**
9. Puerto Rico is the farthest east of all the islands. **Yes** **No**
10. Guadeloupe is part of the Bahamas. **Yes** **No**

B. On the map on the other page, color the islands that make up the Greater Antilles. Then write a caption for the three regions of the Caribbean.

Name ____________________

The Caribbean

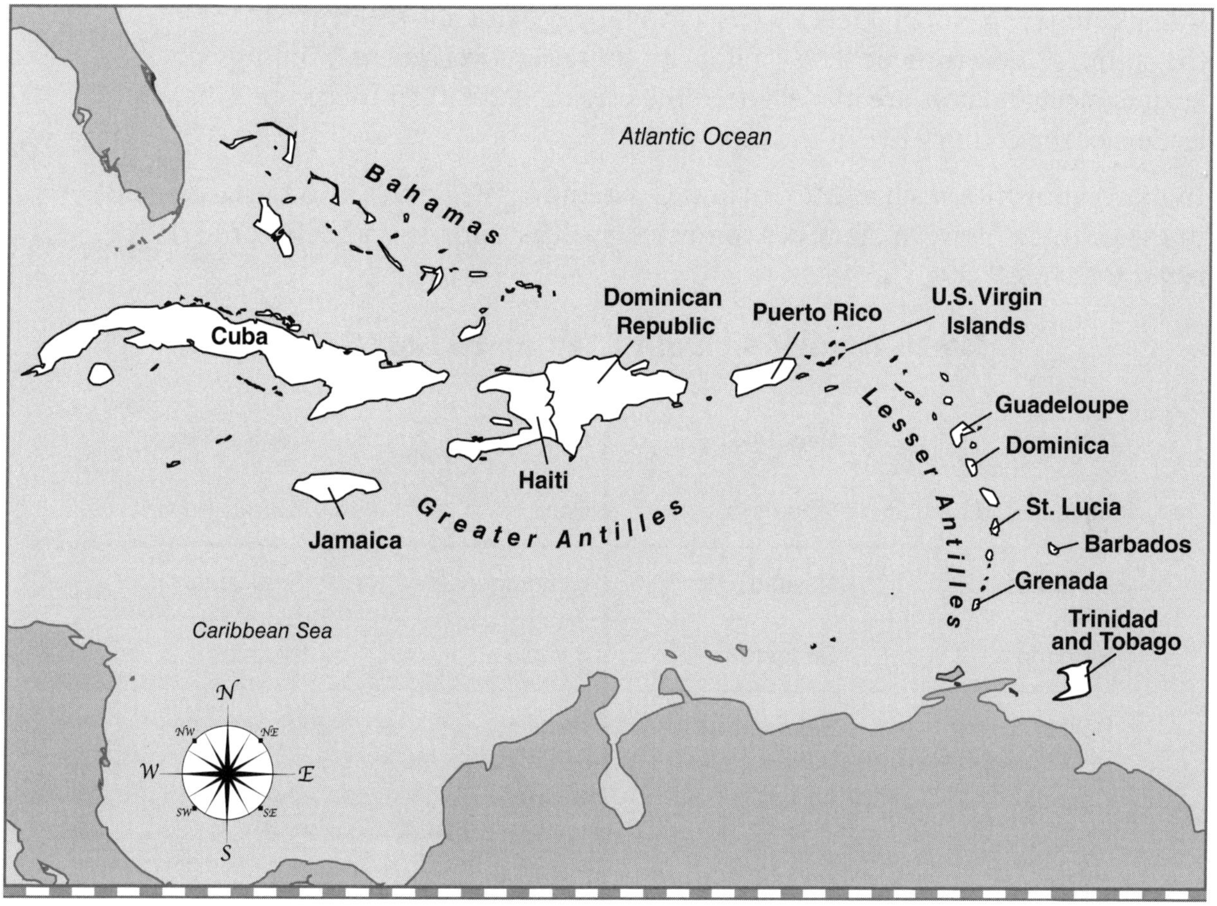
Atlantic Ocean
Bahamas
Cuba
Dominican Republic
Puerto Rico
U.S. Virgin Islands
Haiti
Jamaica
Greater Antilles
Lesser Antilles
Guadeloupe
Dominica
St. Lucia
Barbados
Grenada
Trinidad and Tobago
Caribbean Sea
N
NW
NE
W
E
SW
SE
S

Capital Cities of North America

Every country in North America has a capital city, which is the central location of the country's government. The capital city contains government buildings where leaders meet and laws are made. Often the president, prime minister, or other leaders of the country live in the capital city.

In many countries, such as Mexico and Cuba, the capital city is also the largest city in the country. However, in other countries, such as Canada and Belize, the capital is *not* the largest city.

North American Countries and Their Capitals

Country	Capital City	Country	Capital City
Antigua and Barbuda	St. John's	Haiti	Port-au-Prince
Bahamas	Nassau	Honduras	Tegucigalpa
Barbados	Bridgetown	Jamaica	Kingston
Belize	Belmopan	Mexico	Mexico City
Canada	Ottawa	Nicaragua	Managua
Costa Rica	San José	Panama	Panama City
Cuba	Havana	St. Kitts and Nevis	Basseterre
Dominica	Roseau	St. Lucia	Castries
Dominican Republic	Santo Domingo	St. Vincent and the Grenadines	Kingstown
El Salvador	San Salvador	Trinidad and Tobago	Port-of-Spain
Grenada	St. George's	United States	Washington, D.C.
Guatemala	Guatemala City		

Name ______________________________

Capital Cities of North America

A. Use the chart on the other page to write the capital city that goes with each country.

Costa Rica: ____________________

Barbados: ____________________

Canada: ____________________

Belize: ____________________

Cuba: ____________________

Bahamas: ____________________

United States: ____________________

Mexico: ____________________

St. Lucia: ____________________

Nicaragua: ____________________

Jamaica: ____________________

Honduras: ____________________

B. In the word puzzle, find and circle the 12 capital cities you wrote above. Words may appear across, down, and diagonally.

T	E	G	U	C	I	G	A	L	P	A	B	M
B	S	O	M	A	N	A	G	U	A	B	R	E
E	A	Q	T	Z	A	L	Y	V	K	M	I	X
L	N	U	D	T	L	U	S	W	I	H	D	I
M	J	G	W	N	A	B	U	A	N	P	G	C
O	O	V	M	S	P	W	N	H	G	D	E	O
P	S	P	S	C	S	I	A	A	S	L	T	C
A	E	A	R	X	C	Q	N	S	T	M	O	I
N	N	M	A	N	A	A	U	M	O	T	W	T
W	A	U	O	N	V	V	M	X	N	W	N	Y
P	S	C	A	A	C	A	S	T	R	I	E	S
W	A	S	H	I	N	G	T	O	N	D	C	W

Name ________________________________

Review

Use words from the box to complete the crossword puzzle.

- Canada
- capital
- Caribbean
- continent
- continental
- New York
- population
- seven
- twenty-three

Across

2. the largest North American country in size
7. the number of countries in North America
8. The ____ of Canada is less than Mexico.

Down

1. Washington, D.C., is the ____ of the U.S.
2. a region made up of many islands
3. Hawaii is not part of the ____ U.S.
4. North America is the third-largest ____.
5. the number of countries in Central America
6. the largest U.S. city

SECTION 3

Physical Features of North America

In this section, students learn about the landforms and bodies of water of North America. They discover that North America is home to some of the most dramatic landforms on Earth, including the Grand Canyon and the Rocky Mountains. Students learn about North America's hot deserts and cold northern tundra and also become familiar with the major lakes and rivers in North America.

Each skill in this section is based on the following National Geography Standards:

Essential Element 2: Places and Regions

Standard 4: The physical and human characteristics of places

Essential Element 3: Physical Systems

Standards 7 & 8: The physical processes that shape the patterns of Earth's surface, and the characteristics and spatial distribution of ecosystems on Earth's surface

CONTENTS

Overview

North America is the world's third-largest continent. It is almost completely surrounded by water and is connected to South America by only a thin strip of land. North America has many spectacular natural features.

Landforms

Because of North America's large size, it has a variety of diverse landforms, from island volcanoes to frozen tundra.

Denali

North America has several mountain ranges, the longest of which is the Rocky Mountains. Many of the peaks in the Rocky Mountains are over 14,000 feet (4,267 m) tall! However, the tallest mountain in North America is not located in the Rocky Mountains. It is Alaska's Denali, which is 20,320 feet (6,194 m) tall.

North America has four major deserts. They are the Chihuahuan, Sonoran, Mojave, and Great Basin. These deserts are located in the southwest United States and Mexico. Three of them are hot deserts, while one, the Great Basin Desert, is a cold desert.

Other landforms include grassy plains in the central United States, huge evergreen forests, which cover much of Canada, and tropical rainforests in Central America. Very little grows in the far northern part of the continent, where the land is frozen tundra.

North America is also home to many islands, including the Caribbean islands in the southeast. Several of these islands have active volcanoes.

Bodies of Water

North America is bordered by the Arctic, Pacific, and Atlantic oceans. It is also bordered by many seas, including the frigid Bering, Beaufort, and Labrador seas to the north, and the warm Caribbean Sea to the south. In addition, there are several large gulfs and bays bordering the continent.

North America is also home to the Great Lakes, which make up the largest system of freshwater lakes in the world. About one-fifth of the world's fresh water supply is in the Great Lakes.

There are also many rivers in North America. At 2,500 miles (4,023 km) long, the Missouri River is the longest river on the continent. Together the Missouri, Mississippi, and Ohio rivers make up the third-largest river system in the world.

Overview

Fill in the bubble to answer each question.

1. Which statement is *not* true?
   Ⓐ Denali is over 20,000 feet tall.
   Ⓑ Denali is in the Rocky Mountains.
   Ⓒ Denali is the tallest mountain in North America.
   Ⓓ Denali is in Alaska.

2. Which of these is *not* a desert in North America?
   Ⓐ Great Basin
   Ⓑ Sonoran
   Ⓒ Mojave
   Ⓓ Sahara

3. Which three oceans border North America?
   Ⓐ Pacific, Atlantic, Indian
   Ⓑ Pacific, Indian, Arctic
   Ⓒ Pacific, Atlantic, Arctic
   Ⓓ Atlantic, Arctic, Indian

4. About how much of the world's supply of fresh water is in the Great Lakes?
   Ⓐ 1/4
   Ⓑ 1/5
   Ⓒ 1/6
   Ⓓ 1/10

5. Which of these is the longest river in North America?
   Ⓐ Missouri
   Ⓑ Mississippi
   Ⓒ Ohio
   Ⓓ Denali

North America's Landscape

North America has a varied landscape. There are frozen tundras in the far north, where the land is covered in snow and ice for much of the year. There are tall mountains in the west and hot deserts in the southwest. Coniferous forests dominate the northern central area around Hudson Bay. In the midwest of the United States, the land features flat plains.

A. Study the physical map of North America on the other page. Use the map and key to answer the questions.

1. Which mountain range is along the northwestern coast of North America? ______________________
2. Which mountain range is farthest south? ______________________
3. What is the name of the major mountain peak shown on the map? ______________________
4. Which landform covers most of the central United States? ______________________
5. Which island is north of Hudson Bay? ______________________
6. Which desert is farthest north? ______________________
7. What is the name of the area that surrounds Hudson Bay? ______________________
8. Which peninsula is west of the Caribbean Sea? ______________________

B. Follow the directions to color the map on the other page.

1. Color the deserts yellow.
2. Color the mountains brown.
3. Use light green to circle the plains.
4. Use dark green to circle the Canadian Shield.

North America's Landscape

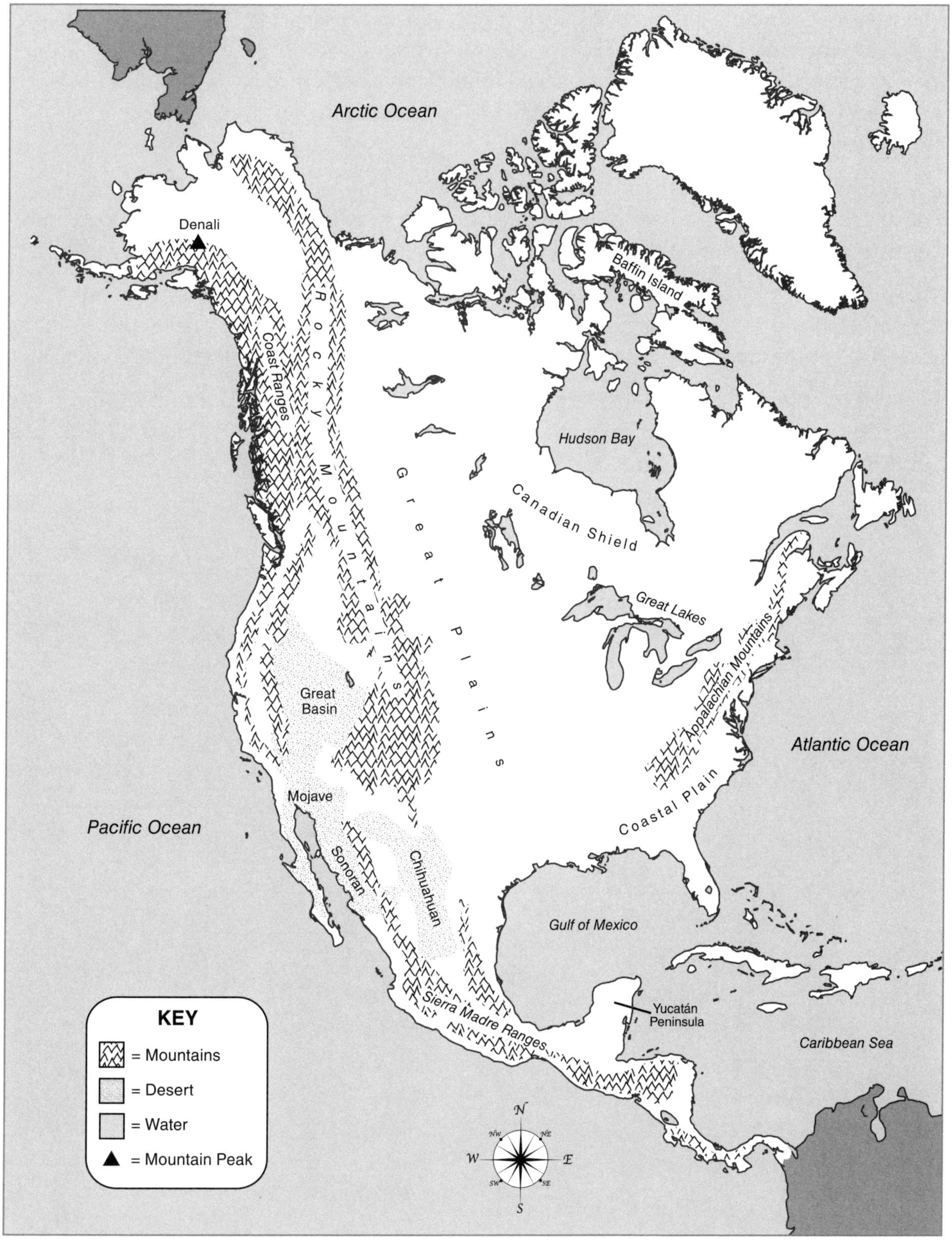
Arctic Ocean
Denali
Baffin Island
Coast Ranges
Rocky Mountains
Great Plains
Hudson Bay
Canadian Shield
Great Lakes
Appalachian Mountains
Great Basin
Atlantic Ocean
Mojave
Coastal Plain
Pacific Ocean
Sonoran
Chihuahuan
Gulf of Mexico
Sierra Madre Ranges
Yucatán Peninsula
Caribbean Sea
KEY
= Mountains
= Desert
= Water
= Mountain Peak
N
NW
NE
W
E
SW
SE
S

Rocky Mountains

The Rocky Mountains (also called "the Rockies") form the largest mountain system in North America. They stretch more than 3,000 miles (4,800 km), from Yukon in northern Canada through the western United States to New Mexico in the south. The Rocky Mountain system is actually made up of over one hundred smaller mountain ranges.

The Rocky Mountains form the Continental Divide. This means that rivers on the west side of the mountains flow west into the Pacific Ocean, while those on the east side flow east into the Atlantic or Arctic oceans.

Many different kinds of animals live on the lower slopes of the Rockies. Only a few animals that can survive in a harsh climate live above the timberline, where trees do not grow. Two of these hardy animals are the Rocky Mountain goat and the bighorn sheep.

At 14,443 feet (4,402 m), Mount Elbert is the highest of the Rocky Mountains. But Mount Elbert has plenty of company. Twenty-four other mountains are over 14,000 feet (4,267 m) tall. All of these mountains are located in the state of Colorado.

Tallest Mountains of the Rockies
(listed in alphabetical order)

Mountain Peak	Height in Feet (Meters)
Blanca Peak	14,345 feet (4,372 m)
Crestone Peak	14,294 feet (4,357 m)
Grays Peak	14,270 feet (4,349 m)
La Plata Peak	14,361 feet (4,377 m)
Mt. Antero	14,269 feet (4,349 m)
Mt. Elbert	14,443 feet (4,402 m)
Mt. Harvard	14,420 feet (4,395 m)
Mt. Lincoln	14,286 feet (4,354 m)
Mt. Massive	14,421 feet (4,396 m)
Uncompahgre Peak	14,309 feet (4,361 m)

Rocky Mountains

A. Read each statement. Circle **yes** if it is true or **no** if it is false. Use the information on the other page to help you.

1.	The Rocky Mountain system is over 3,000 miles long.	**Yes**	**No**
2.	The Rocky Mountains are in the eastern United States.	**Yes**	**No**
3.	The Continental Divide determines the direction in which rivers flow.	**Yes**	**No**
4.	Mount Massive is the tallest mountain in the Rockies.	**Yes**	**No**
5.	Mount Elbert is over 14,500 feet tall.	**Yes**	**No**
6.	Mount Elbert is located in the state of Wyoming.	**Yes**	**No**
7.	Bighorn sheep live above the timberline in the Rocky Mountains.	**Yes**	**No**
8.	Blanca Peak is 14,345 feet tall.	**Yes**	**No**
9.	La Plata Peak is taller than Mount Harvard.	**Yes**	**No**
10.	Grays Peak is only a foot taller than Mount Antero.	**Yes**	**No**

B. Use the chart on the other page to write the names of the 10 tallest mountains in the Rockies, from largest to smallest.

Rank	Mountain Peak
1	
2	
3	
4	
5	

Rank	Mountain Peak
6	
7	
8	
9	
10	

Grand Canyon

The Grand Canyon, located in northwest Arizona, is one of the largest canyons on Earth. It is 277 miles (446 km) long and about a mile (1.6 km) deep. The width of the canyon varies. In some spots it is less than a mile wide, while in others it is 18 miles (29 km) across.

The Grand Canyon was formed by a process called erosion. Over millions of years, the Colorado River, which runs through the canyon, wore away at the layers of rock to carve out the canyon. Some of the types of rocks that make up the Grand Canyon include sandstone, shale, and limestone. These different rock layers can be clearly seen in the canyon walls. Most are various shades of red, but there are also shades of brown, gray, pink, and green.

The canyon includes many smaller gorges and ravines, as well as interesting plants and wildlife. There are several kinds of trees, including ponderosa pine, juniper, aspen, fir, and spruce. The cactus plant is also plentiful. Over 300 different species of birds have been spotted at the Grand Canyon. There are also elk, deer, mountain lions, and several types of lizards and snakes, including the poisonous Grand Canyon pink rattlesnake, which is found nowhere else in the world.

Millions of people visit the Grand Canyon each year. Most are content to view the canyon from the rim. But some people hike or ride donkeys down to the bottom. Still others raft through the canyon on the Colorado River.

Grand Canyon

A. Use the information on the other page to help you answer the questions.

1. In what state is the Grand Canyon located? ____________________
2. How long is the Grand Canyon? ____________________
3. About how deep is the Grand Canyon? ____________________
4. What are three types of rock that can be found in the Grand Canyon?

   ____
5. In your own words, describe how the Grand Canyon was formed.

   ____

   ____

B. Pretend you are going to the bottom of the Grand Canyon. Answer the questions about how you will plan your trip. Use the information on the other page to help you.

1. Will you hike, ride, or raft to the bottom of the canyon? Why did you choose that way?

   ____

   ____
2. What are four things that you will need to bring with you?

   ____

   ____
3. Name two things you would like to see and do on a visit to the Grand Canyon.

   ____

   ____

Deserts of North America

There are four major deserts in North America. They are the Chihuahuan, Sonoran, Mojave, and Great Basin deserts. These deserts are connected to each other and cover a large area of the southwestern United States and Mexico.

Because these areas get very little rain—usually under 10 inches (25 cm) a year—plants must be hardy in order to survive. However, a surprising number of plants thrive in the desert environment, including sagebrush, creosote bush, agave, yucca, and cactuses. These plants provide food and protection for many desert animals. Coyotes, jack rabbits, bighorn sheep, pocket mice, rattlesnakes, Gila monsters, and roadrunners are a few of the animals that make the desert their home.

Even though all four of North America's major deserts are located in the southwestern part of the continent, they are each different in size, climate, and plant life. The climate of a desert is determined by where it is located on the continent and by its *elevation*, or height above sea level. Deserts that are farther south and lower in elevation will be warmer. Deserts that are located farther north and at higher elevations will be cooler.

The Four Deserts of North America

Desert	Size	Interesting Facts
Chihuahuan	175,000 sq. miles (453,000 sq. km)	This vast, mountainous desert is located on a high plateau. It is covered with stones and sandy soil. The number of different plants that grow in the Chihuahuan is not high. Yuccas, agave, and cactuses are common.
Great Basin	190,000 sq. miles (492,000 sq. km)	The Great Basin Desert is a cool desert because it is farther north on the continent and because it is located at a high elevation. The terrain includes areas with mountains, as well as flat salt beds.
Mojave	25,000 sq. miles (65,000 sq. km)	This desert includes Death Valley, where it gets extremely hot, as well as cooler areas farther north. The Joshua tree can be found only in the Mojave. There are also many unique rock formations.
Sonoran	120,000 sq. miles (311,000 sq. km)	Located far to the south and low in elevation, the Sonoran desert is the hottest of the North American deserts. The Sonoran also gets more rain than the other North American deserts.

Deserts of North America

Circle the answer that completes each sentence. Use the information on the other page to help you.

1.	The four major deserts are mostly in the ____.	**southwest**	**southeast**
2.	An agave is ____.	**a plant**	**an animal**
3.	An animal that lives in the desert is the ____.	**lemming**	**pocket mouse**
4.	The ____ is a cool desert.	**Chihuahuan**	**Great Basin**
5.	Death Valley is in the ____ Desert.	**Mojave**	**Sonoran**
6.	Joshua trees can be found in the ____.	**Great Basin**	**Mojave**
7.	The ____ is the hottest desert.	**Chihuahuan**	**Sonoran**
8.	The ____ is located on a plateau.	**Chihuahuan**	**Mojave**
9.	The ____ is the biggest desert.	**Great Basin**	**Sonoran**
10.	The ____ desert covers 120,000 square miles.	**Chihuahuan**	**Sonoran**

Frozen North

The northern regions of North America are very cold. They stretch all the way into the Arctic Circle, which is an area that surrounds the North Pole. In the winter, temperatures in the northern part of the continent may reach as low as –58°F (–50°C). The land in the coldest regions of the north is called *tundra*, meaning that the ground there is permanently frozen. In this environment, no trees and only a few stout plants can grow. In the areas closest to the Arctic Circle, nothing grows at all.

Although the entire north is very cold, different regions of the north have different landscapes. Parts of Alaska and the northwestern part of Canada are mountainous with many glaciers. Closer to Hudson Bay in the east, there are large *coniferous* forests. Conifers are trees such as pines, spruces, and firs that have needles for leaves. This type of landscape is called *taiga*, or *boreal forest*. The area has cold, snowy winters and short, warmer summers. Around the Hudson Bay, there are also very rocky areas with many lakes. This area is called the Canadian Shield.

To the far north, the Arctic Islands are cold and barren. Some have mountains, while others are flat. Many of these islands are unexplored. Greenland is the largest island in the world, but few people live there due to the harsh climate. About 80% of the island is covered in a mile-thick (1.6 km) sheet of ice.

A. Use the information above to answer the questions.

1. What is a tundra?

____

____

2. What is a taiga?

____

____

3. Why don't many people live in Greenland?

____

____

Frozen North

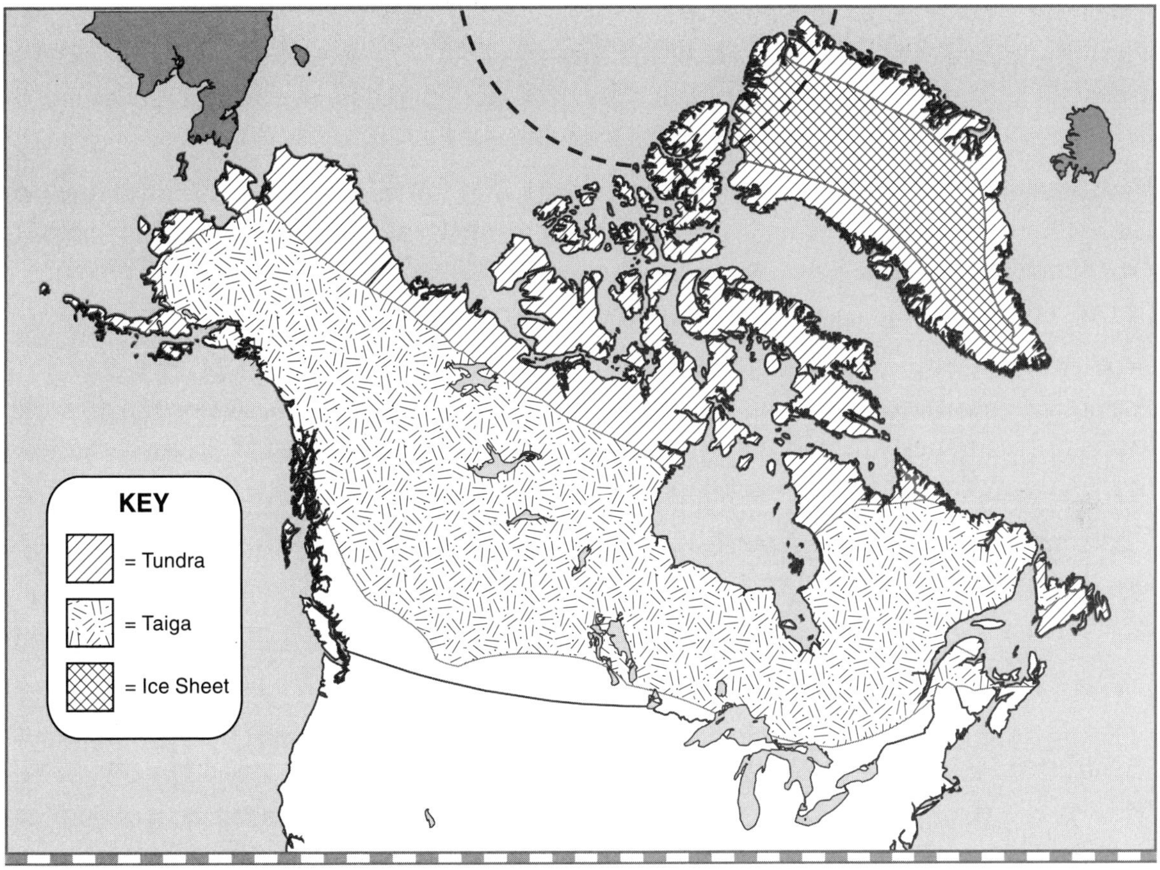

B. Follow the directions to color the map.

1. Color the taiga region green.
2. Color the tundra purple.
3. Color the ice sheet gray.
4. Use red to trace the dotted line (Arctic Circle).

Central America's Rainforests

Rainforests cover about 86,000 square miles (222,739 square km) of Central America. That's roughly the size of the state of Minnesota. That may seem like a lot, but sadly, large areas of Central America's rainforests have been destroyed. El Salvador is the most deforested country in Central America, with 85% of its rainforest destroyed.

Rainforests in Central America have been destroyed for many reasons. Many have been logged for timber, both legally and illegally. In other areas, the land has been cleared to grow crops or to create pasture land for raising cattle. Some rainforests have also been destroyed by mining, road construction, and forest fires.

Tropical rainforests are home to millions of plants and animals. In the tiny Central American country of Costa Rica alone, there are about 12,000 kinds of plants and 1,200 kinds of butterflies! Unfortunately, many of these plants and animals are endangered due to illegal hunting and the loss of habitat.

Fortunately, some Central American rainforests are protected by the government. Environmental groups are working hard to save the others.

Central American Rainforest

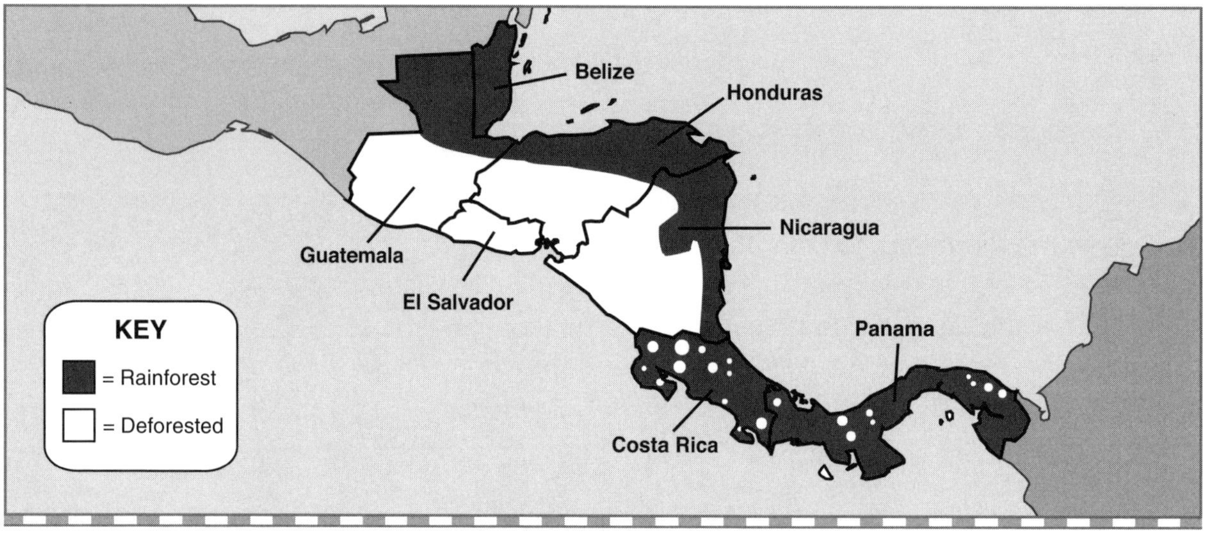

A. Write four reasons that rainforests in Central America have been destroyed.

1. ______________________
2. ______________________
3. ______________________
4. ______________________

Name ____________________

Central America's Rainforests

B. Use the information on the other page to complete the secret code. Read each clue below and write the answer. Then use the numbers to crack the code!

1. Many of the tropical rainforests in Central America have been ____.

   10 11 25 26 24 21 5 11 10

2. El Salvador has lost 85 ____ of its rainforest.

   22 11 24 9 11 20 26

3. Trees are often cut down and logged for ____.

   26 15 19 8 11 24

4. Many rainforests have been cleared to make ____ land for raising cattle.

   22 7 25 26 1 24 11

5. There are about 12,000 different ____ of plants in Costa Rica.

   17 15 20 10 25

6. Some Central American rainforests are protected by the ____.

   14 21 23 11 24 20 19 11 20 26

Crack the Code!

Several species of Central and South American ____ are endangered.

25 22 15 10 11 24   19 21 20 17 11 5 25

Islands of the Caribbean

The Caribbean Sea and the Atlantic Ocean are separated by a chain of islands called the Caribbean islands, or West Indies. This island chain is over 2,000 miles (3,200 km) long and stretches from the tip of Florida to the northern coast of Venezuela in South America.

There are thousands of islands in the Caribbean island chain. The islands are part of an ancient underwater mountain range that stretched between North and South America. Many of the islands were once the peaks of mountains. Over millions of years, the peaks were worn away by the wind and rain. Other islands were formed when volcanoes erupted below the sea. There are still live volcanoes on several of the Caribbean islands.

The Caribbean islands are located over the intersection of several *tectonic plates*. Tectonic plates are large sections of Earth's crust. These massive plates move slowly into or away from each other, plunging the edge of one plate under the other, or ripping the crust apart. Movement of the tectonic plates often results in violent natural disasters, such as earthquakes, tsunamis (large ocean waves), and volcanic eruptions. Earthquakes and volcanic eruptions are still common on the Caribbean islands. For example, a 7.0 magnitude earthquake struck the Caribbean nation of Haiti in 2010, killing more than 200,000 people.

Tectonic Plates

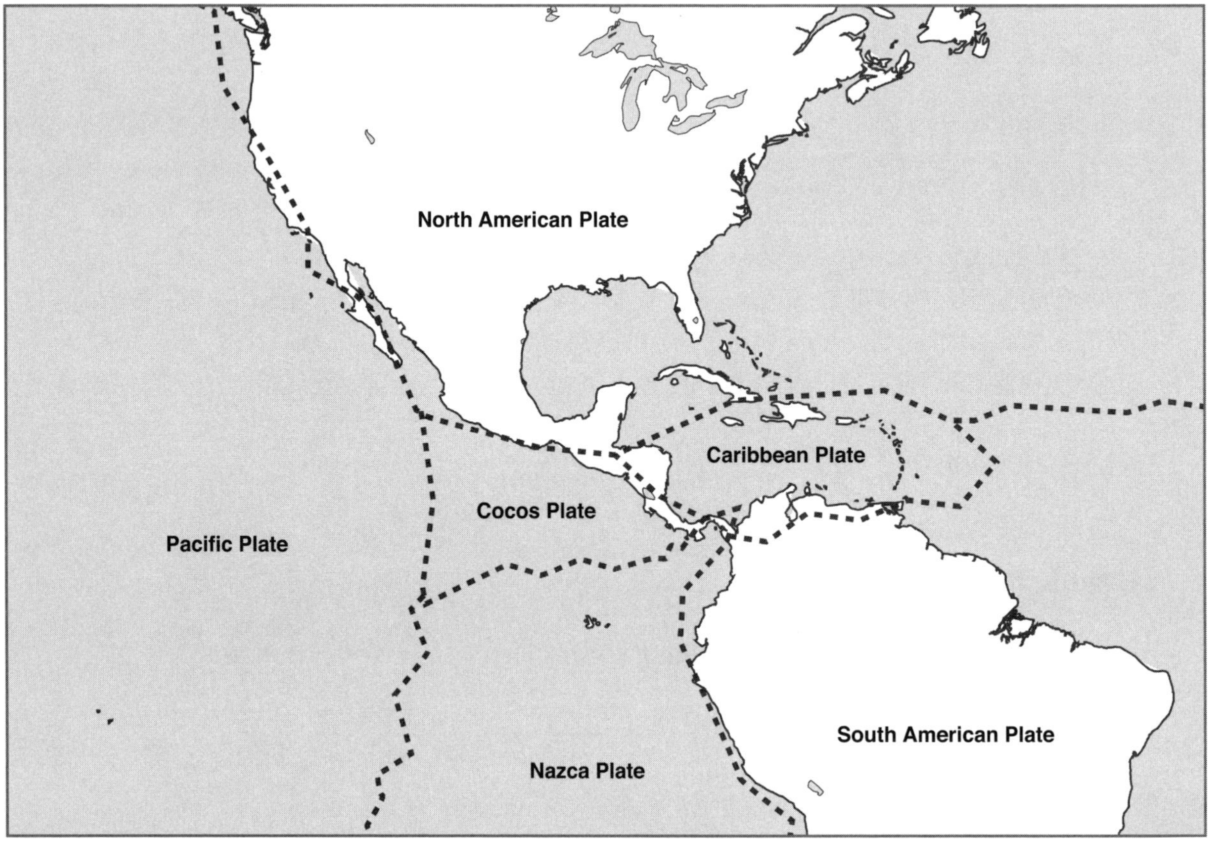

Name ______________________________

Islands of the Caribbean

Circle the answer that completes each sentence. Use information from the other page and the chart of Caribbean volcanoes below to help you.

Volcano	Island	Last Eruption
Soufrière Hills	Montserrat	2010
Soufrière Guadeloupe	Guadeloupe	1977
Morne Watt	Dominica	1997
Pelée	Martinique	1932
Qualibou	St. Lucia	1766
Soufrière St. Vincent	St. Vincent	1979
Kick 'em Jenny	Grenada*	2001

*Located off the coast of Grenada

1. Some of the Caribbean islands were formed by ____.

   earthquakes **tsunamis** **volcanoes**

2. A tectonic plate is a large piece of the Earth's ____.

   crust **continent** **core**

3. Most of the Caribbean islands are on the Caribbean and ____ plates.

   South American **North American** **Cocos**

4. The most recent Caribbean volcanic eruption was on the island of ____.

   Dominica **Grenada** **Montserrat**

5. ____ Caribbean volcanoes have erupted in the last hundred years.

   six **seven** **nine**

6. Kick 'em Jenny is near the island of ____.

   St. Lucia **Dominica** **Grenada**

7. Qualibou erupted in ____.

   1766 **1979** **1932**

North America's Bodies of Water

North America is bordered by three oceans. They are the Pacific, Atlantic, and Arctic. However, there are also many seas, gulfs, and bays that surround North America. For example, the Caribbean Sea is a part of the Atlantic Ocean that surrounds the Caribbean islands in southeastern North America. The Gulf of California is a small sliver of the Pacific Ocean that separates Baja California from mainland Mexico. And the Hudson Bay is a portion of the northern Atlantic Ocean that cuts into Canada.

North America also contains several long rivers and large lakes. The Mississippi River system in the United States is one of the largest river systems in the world. It includes the Mississippi, Missouri, and Ohio rivers. Lake Superior, one of the Great Lakes that separate the U.S. and Canada, is the largest freshwater lake on the planet.

A. Look at the map on the other page. Match each body of water below to the corresponding number on the map. Then label the body of water on the map.

1. Arctic Ocean
2. Atlantic Ocean
3. Pacific Ocean
4. Gulf of Mexico
5. Gulf of California
6. Caribbean Sea
7. Hudson Bay
8. Lake Superior

B. Use the information above and the map on the other page to answer the questions.

1. Which bay is farthest north? ____________________
2. Which body of water separates two areas of Mexico? ____________________
3. What ocean is the Caribbean Sea connected to? ____________________
4. What is the northernmost gulf in the United States? ____________________
5. Which bay separates Canada and Greenland? ____________________

Name ______________________

North America's Bodies of Water

Great Lakes

The Great Lakes are located on the border between Canada and the United States. Of the five lakes, only Lake Michigan is completely within the United States. The other four lakes help form the border between the United States and Canada.

The Great Lakes were formed during the last ice age, about 10,000 years ago. Huge sheets of ice, called *glaciers*, covered Canada and the northern United States. When the glaciers receded, they left ridges and large basins. Some of the water from the melting glaciers filled in these basins, creating the lakes.

The Great Lakes and the channels that connect them form the largest fresh-water system on Earth. They hold about one-fifth of the world's supply of fresh water. If the water from the Great Lakes was spread evenly over the United States (not including Alaska and Hawaii), the entire country would be covered in nearly 10 feet of water!

Lake Superior is the largest and deepest of the Great Lakes. It is also the coldest lake. Lake Ontario is the smallest lake, but it actually contains four times as much water as Lake Erie, which is about 2,600 square miles larger than Lake Ontario. That is because Lake Erie is very shallow. Since it is so shallow, Lake Erie warms up quickly in summer. It is more likely to freeze in winter than the other Great Lakes.

The Five Great Lakes

Great Lake	Size	Average Depth	Maximum Depth
Erie	9,900 sq. miles (25,700 sq. km)	62 feet (19 m)	210 feet (64 m)
Huron	23,000 sq. miles (59,600 sq. km)	195 feet (59 m)	750 feet (229 m)
Michigan	22,300 sq. miles (57,800 sq. km)	279 feet (85 m)	925 feet (282 m)
Ontario	7,300 sq. miles (19,000 sq. km)	283 feet (86 m)	802 feet (244 m)
Superior	31,700 sq. miles (82,100 sq. km)	483 feet (147 m)	1,332 feet (406 m)

A. Write a caption for the map on the other page to compare at least two of the lakes. Use the information on this page to help you.

Great Lakes

____

____

B. Circle the lake that matches each clue. Use the information on the other page and the map above to help you.

1. the largest lake	**Lake Superior**	**Lake Michigan**
2. the shallowest lake	**Lake Erie**	**Lake Ontario**
3. the smallest lake	**Lake Erie**	**Lake Ontario**
4. the second-largest lake	**Lake Michigan**	**Lake Huron**
5. the only lake completely in the U.S.	**Lake Michigan**	**Lake Huron**
6. the coldest lake	**Lake Ontario**	**Lake Superior**
7. the lake with an average depth of 283 feet	**Lake Erie**	**Lake Ontario**
8. the lake that has an area of 22,300 square miles	**Lake Superior**	**Lake Michigan**

North America's Rivers

There are hundreds of rivers in North America. Rivers are an important source of fresh water. Farmers use rivers to irrigate crops. Rivers provide important transportation routes for goods and people. Rivers can also be used to produce *hydroelectricity*, which is electricity that is produced by the energy of running water.

The Missouri River is the longest river in North America. It is 2,500 miles (4,023 km) long. The Missouri River and the Ohio River are tributaries of the mighty Mississippi River. That means that they flow into the Mississippi. Together, these three rivers make up the third-largest river system in the world.

In Canada, the St. Lawrence River connects the Great Lakes to the Atlantic Ocean. It is an important waterway for transporting goods.

The Rio Grande River forms most of the border between Texas and Mexico. And in Central America, the longest river is the Rio Coco. It forms much of the boundary between Honduras and Nicaragua.

A. This map shows 12 major rivers in North America. Write the numbers **1** through **5** to label the five longest rivers in order from longest to shortest. Use the chart on the other page to help you.

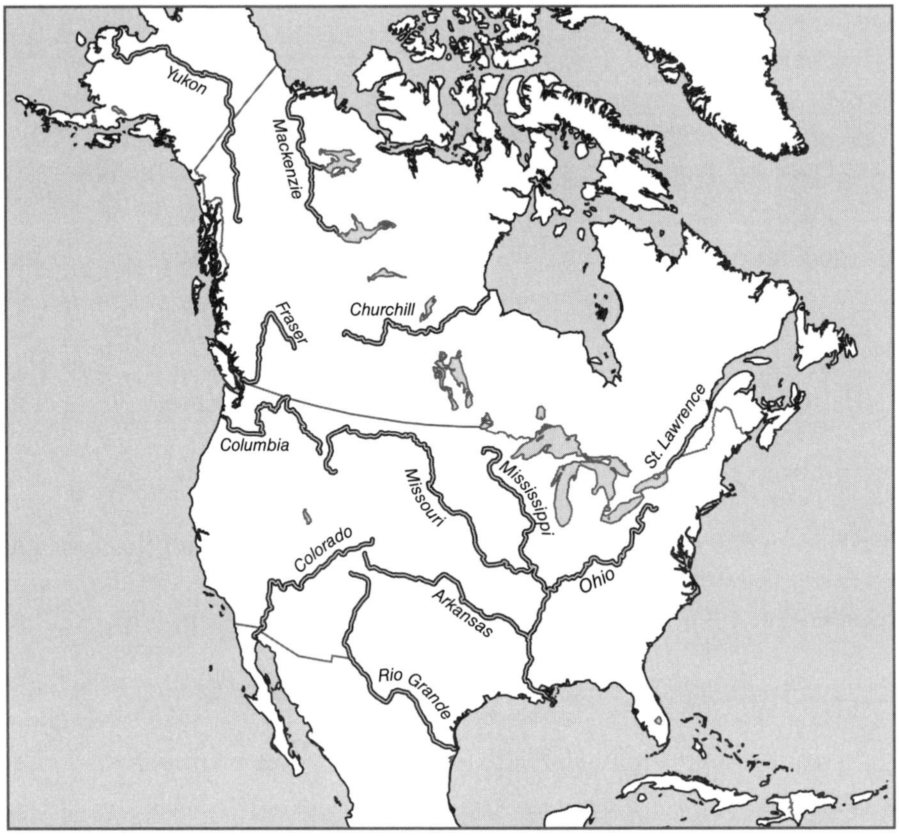

North America's Rivers

River	Length in Miles (Kilometers)
Arkansas	1,460 miles (2,350 km)
Churchill	1,000 miles (1,609 km)
Colorado	1,450 miles (2,333 km)
Columbia	1,152 miles (1,854 km)
Fraser	850 miles (1,368 km)
Mackenzie	1,200 miles (1,931 km)
Mississippi	2,339 miles (3,765 km)
Missouri	2,500 miles (4,023 km)
Ohio	975 miles (1,569 km)
Rio Grande	1,885 miles (3,034 km)
St. Lawrence	760 miles (1,223 km)
Yukon	1,980 miles (2,036 km)

B. In the word puzzle, find and circle the names of the rivers from above. Words may appear across, down, or diagonally.

F	C	O	L	O	R	A	D	O	Y	P	E	L	R	E
S	O	R	A	T	J	M	E	W	F	A	D	Q	U	I
T	L	I	R	X	M	L	A	L	P	R	N	A	B	N
L	U	C	K	E	I	Z	N	E	K	I	A	M	Z	C
A	M	O	A	A	S	B	S	L	I	O	R	S	O	H
W	B	R	N	T	S	A	V	R	B	G	G	M	E	U
R	I	W	S	E	I	Q	U	U	M	R	O	M	L	R
E	A	O	A	C	S	O	U	L	K	A	I	R	E	C
N	R	T	S	A	S	M	O	L	Z	N	R	M	C	H
C	E	V	O	S	I	R	U	O	S	D	I	M	P	I
E	Z	I	I	K	P	B	N	S	H	E	E	P	X	L
A	H	M	N	I	P	N	Y	U	K	O	N	L	M	L
O	K	H	O	T	I	M	A	C	K	E	N	Z	I	E

Panama Canal

The Panama Canal was one of the most ambitious building projects in human history. It was cut through the narrowest part of Central America to connect the Pacific and Atlantic oceans. Before the construction of the canal in 1914, ships had to sail all the way around South America. That meant an extra 8,000 miles (12,800 km) for a ship to sail from New York to San Francisco.

The canal is 51 miles (82 km) long and 10 miles (16 km) wide. It takes nine hours to make the crossing. The reason it takes so long is that the canal was cut through land that is about 85 feet (26 m) above sea level. So ships must be raised up to this level when they enter the canal, and lowered back down when they exit. This is done with a series of *locks*, or sections of water with gates between them. When the gates are opened or closed, water flows in and out, raising and lowering the boat on the water. About 40 ships cross each day. That's about 14,000 ships each year.

Facts About the Panama Canal

- France was the first country to attempt building the canal in the late 1800s. The French failed, and nearly 20,000 workers lost their lives, most to tropical diseases such as yellow fever and malaria.
- The workers who built the canal had to deal with huge swarms of insects, including mosquitoes that carried dangerous diseases.
- The Panama Canal was finally built by the United States. It took 100,000 workers 11 years to build the canal.
- The official opening of the canal was on August 15, 1914. The *SS Ancon* was the first ship to sail through the canal.
- Although the canal was built by the United States, ownership was returned to Panama in 1999.
- The Panama Canal cost $375 million to build. That is equivalent to $7.5 billion today.
- The gates between the locks have to be strong enough to hold back millions of pounds of water. They are made of steel and are seven feet (2 m) thick. Each of the hinges weighs over 14 tons (12.7 metric tons).
- About 5% of the world's trade goods travel through the Panama Canal.
- Ships must pay a fee to use the canal. An average-sized cargo ship pays about $43,000.

Panama Canal

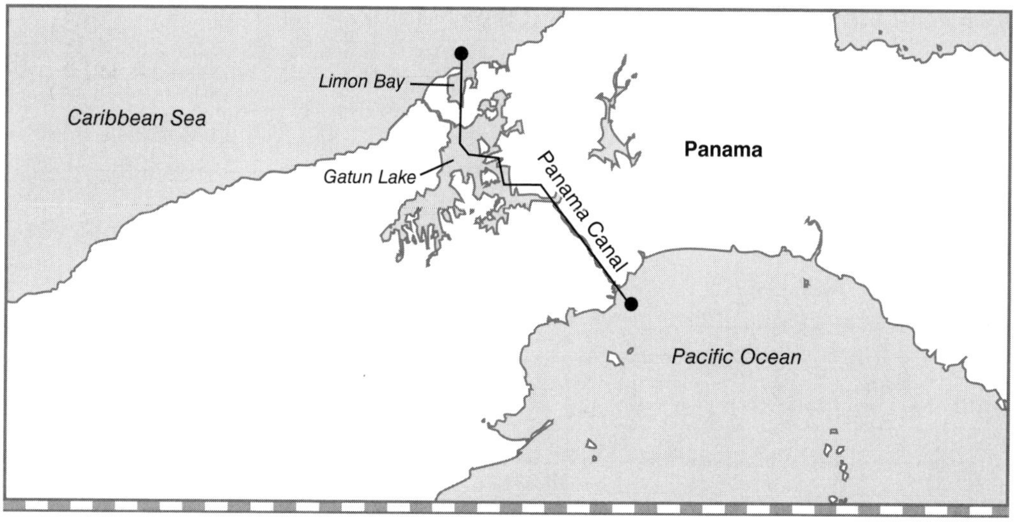

Unscramble the word below each line to complete the sentence. Use the information on the other page to help you.

1. The Panama Canal connects the Pacific and ______________________ oceans.
   ticlanat

2. The Panama Canal is 10 miles ______________________.
   dwie

3. It took ______________________ years to build the canal.
   veenel

4. Workers built a series of ______________________ to lift ships above sea level.
   scolk

5. The ______________________ for the gates of the locks each weigh over 14 tons.
   sheign

6. The first attempt to build the canal was made by ______________________.
   cenfar

7. The Panama Canal officially opened on ______________________ 15, 1914.
   stugua

8. The *SS* ______________________ was the first ship through the Panama Canal.
   conan

Name ______________________

Review

Use words from the box to complete the crossword puzzle.

erosion
Gulf of Mexico
Lake Superior
Missouri
Panama Canal
rainforest
tundra
volcanic

Across

2. an important waterway linking the Atlantic and the Pacific oceans
4. the process that formed the Grand Canyon
5. the longest river in North America
7. the body of water connected to the Caribbean Sea
8. Some Caribbean islands are _____.

Down

1. the largest of the Great Lakes
3. a region of dense vegetation
6. frozen land in the north

SECTION 4

Valuable Resources of North America

In this section, students learn about the various natural resources of North America. They discover that energy production is an important industry on the continent. Students also learn about important regional crops and are introduced to some of the challenges of fishing and logging. In addition, they learn about interesting animals of North America.

Each skill in this section is based on the following National Geography Standards:

Essential Element 3: Physical Systems

Standard 8: The characteristics and spatial distribution of ecosystems on Earth's surface

Essential Element 5: Environment and Society

Standard 14: How human actions modify the physical environment

Standard 16: The changes that occur in the meaning, use, distribution, and importance of resources

CONTENTS

Overview

Natural resources are materials found in nature that people can use. North America is rich in many kinds of natural resources. There are large deposits of fossil fuels, areas of ideal farming soil, abundant fish in the oceans, and extensive forests teeming with plants and animals.

Energy

Oil, natural gas, and coal are important resources in North America. These are all fossil fuels, which take millions of years to form and cannot be replaced. They also cause pollution when burned. Other less-polluting energy resources such as hydropower, wind power, and solar power can never run out, so they are starting to replace the use of some of North America's fossil fuels.

Fishing and Farming

Many people in the coastal communities of North America rely on fishing for their livelihood. Because fish is not a main food source for most North Americans, much of the catch is sent to other countries. However, the fish population of North America's waters has been decreasing significantly due to overfishing.

North America also grows much of the world's supply of corn, soybeans, wheat, coffee, and bananas. Most farms in North America are very large, and many specialize in just one crop.

Forests

Most of Canada and parts of the west coast of the United States are covered by *coniferous*, or evergreen, forests. Other forests of trees such as maple, oak, and birch cover the eastern part of the United States. There are also tropical forests in the southern parts of the continent. These forests are home to many species of plants and animals. However, many of these forests are being cut down for lumber or to make room for croplands and pastures for grazing animals.

Animals

Many wild animals live in North America. Musk oxen and polar bears have thick coats to survive in the cold climate of the northern part of the continent, while humpback whales swim in the freezing Arctic Ocean. The milder climate in the middle of the continent provides the perfect environment for many kinds of mammals, from bison to beavers. Farther south, desert lizards such as the Gila monster thrive in the hot sun, while birds such as the colorful Central American quetzal make their home in the tropical rainforest.

Overview

Fill in the bubble to answer each question or complete each sentence.

1. Which of these resources is *not* a fossil fuel?
   - Ⓐ coal
   - Ⓑ natural gas
   - Ⓒ wind
   - Ⓓ oil

2. Which of these crops was *not* mentioned in the information on the other page?
   - Ⓐ bananas
   - Ⓑ olives
   - Ⓒ soybeans
   - Ⓓ corn

3. Most of Canada is covered by ____.
   - Ⓐ coniferous forests
   - Ⓑ rainforests
   - Ⓒ mountains
   - Ⓓ deserts

4. Which of these animals lives in a hot climate?
   - Ⓐ musk ox
   - Ⓑ Gila monster
   - Ⓒ humpback whale
   - Ⓓ bison

5. Which of these animals lives in the tropical rainforest?
   - Ⓐ beaver
   - Ⓑ Gila monster
   - Ⓒ bison
   - Ⓓ quetzal

Fossil Fuels

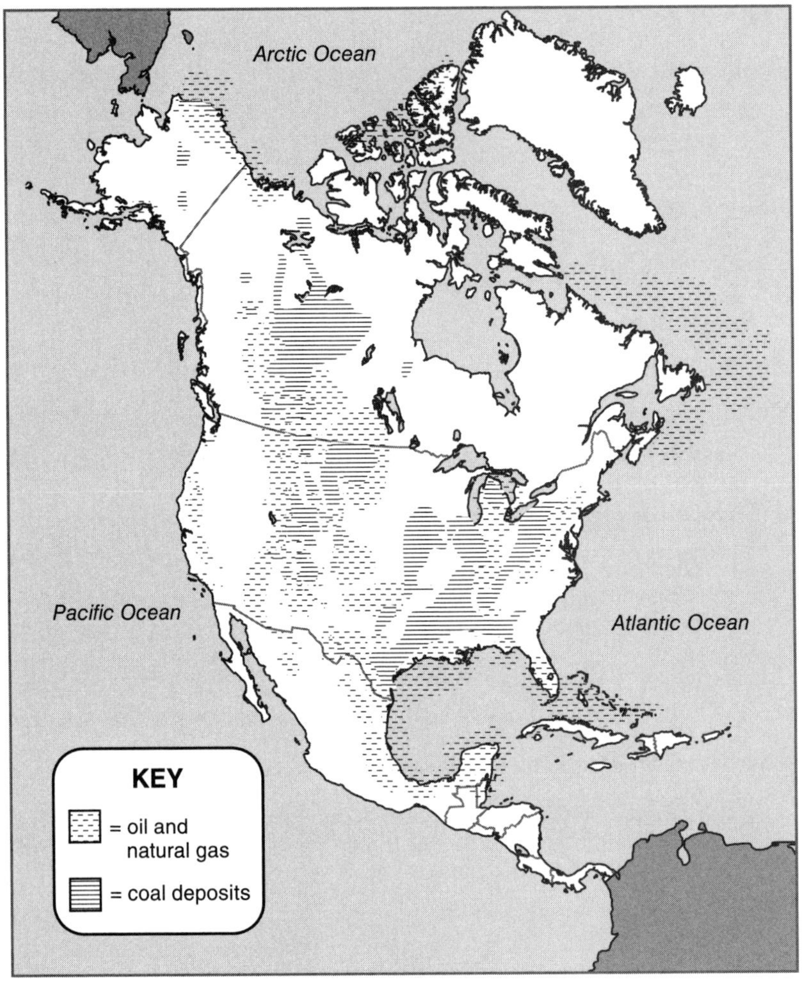

North America is rich in oil, natural gas, and coal. These are all types of fossil fuels. Fossil fuels were formed from the remains of animals and plants that lived millions of years ago. Fossil fuels are *nonrenewable,* meaning they cannot be replaced once they're used up because they take millions of years to form. Over half the energy that the United States and Canada use comes from fossil fuels.

Oil and natural gas are found in large underground deposits and are reached by drilling. Oil is used to make gasoline, diesel fuel, and heating oil. Natural gas is used mainly to heat buildings and for cooking.

Coal is a mineral that is mined using heavy machinery and explosives. It is burned to make electricity and to heat buildings. Unfortunately, burning coal, as well as oil and natural gas, causes pollution that most scientists believe is contributing to global warming. The process of removing coal from the ground can also cause a lot of damage to the environment.

Deposits of oil, natural gas, and coal tend to be found in the same area. There is a great deal of coal in the Appalachian Mountains in the eastern United States and southwest of the Great Lakes. Natural gas can be found in the Gulf of Mexico area, as well as southeast of the Great Lakes. Large oil fields are found off the coast of Alaska and in California, Texas, and Mexico.

Fossil Fuels

A. Read each statement. Circle **yes** if it is true or **no** if it is false. Use the information on the other page to help you.

1. Oil, natural gas, and coal are fossil fuels.	**Yes**	**No**
2. North America will never run out of coal.	**Yes**	**No**
3. Half the energy used in the U.S. comes from natural gas.	**Yes**	**No**
4. Natural gas is used to heat buildings and for cooking.	**Yes**	**No**
5. Coal mining does not do much damage to the land.	**Yes**	**No**
6. Fossil fuels cause pollution.	**Yes**	**No**
7. Fossil fuels take millions of years to form.	**Yes**	**No**
8. People use explosives to find oil.	**Yes**	**No**
9. Coal is burned to make electricity.	**Yes**	**No**
10. People use oil to make gasoline and diesel fuel.	**Yes**	**No**

B. What are two problems associated with using coal for fuel?

1. ____

2. ____

C. Use the map on the other page to help you answer the questions.

1. Which part of the United States has more coal, eastern or western? ______________________

2. In which two oceans are there large deposits of oil and natural gas?

____

Hydroelectricity

The rivers of North America provide an important resource. Water from rivers can be used to generate electricity. This form of energy is called *hydroelectricity*. Hydroelectricity is a renewable resource and is relatively inexpensive to produce. Also, unlike burning fossil fuels, hydroelectricity does not cause pollution.

In order to use water to make electricity, people must construct a dam on a river. A single river may have hundreds of dams along its length. Unfortunately, that can have some negative effects on the environment. Damming a river makes it impossible for migrating fish such as salmon to swim up the river to lay their eggs. It also makes the water warmer, which is not good for plants and animals that are adapted to colder temperatures. In addition, dams cause a buildup of mud and silt, which can clog a river.

About 15% of the world's electricity comes from hydroelectricity. Rivers in the Canadian Shield provide a great deal of hydroelectricity in Quebec and Ontario. The United States has over 2,000 hydroelectric plants. Of these, the Grand Coulee Dam on the Columbia River in Washington produces the most electricity.

Hydroelectricity uses the power of flowing water to create electricity. Here's how it works:

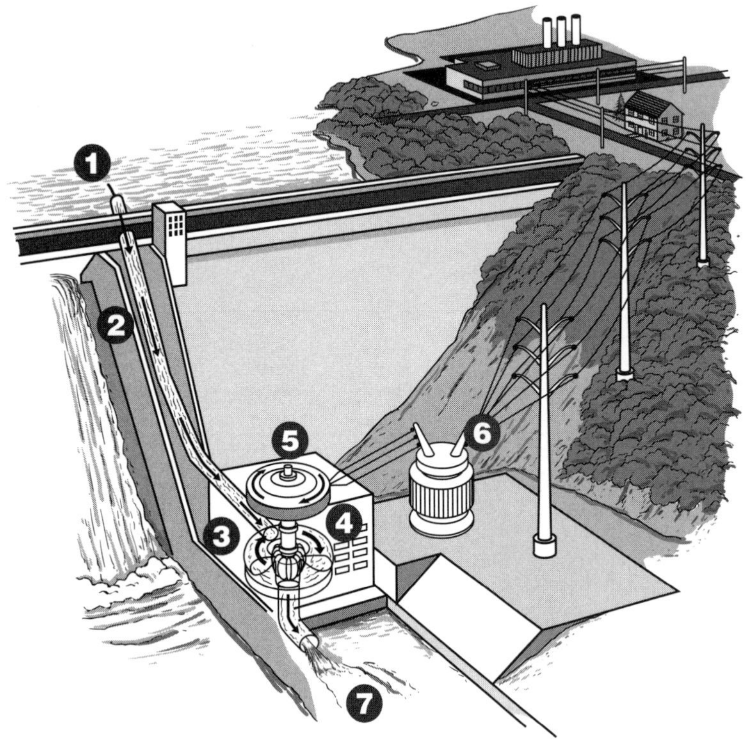

1. Water from behind the dam falls through the floodgates.
2. The water gathers speed as it flows down through a tunnel called a *penstock*.
3. The water hits the blades of a machine called a *turbine*, causing the turbine to spin quickly.
4. The turbine is attached to a shaft. As the turbine spins, so does the shaft.
5. The shaft spins magnets in the generator. This makes electricity in the wire coils that surround the magnets.
6. The electricity is carried away to homes and buildings by the transmission wires.
7. The water flows out of the dam and down the river.

Name ______________________

Hydroelectricity

A. Number the steps for making hydroelectricity in order from **1** to **7**. Use the diagram on the other page to help you.

_____ The water hits the blades of the turbine, making the turbine spin.

_____ The water flows out of the dam and down the river.

_____ Electricity is carried away by the transmission wires.

_____ The shaft spins magnets in the generator to make electricity.

_____ Water comes through the floodgates.

_____ The shaft spins.

_____ The water flows down through the penstock.

B. What are three environmental problems that are caused by dams?

1. ______________________________

2. ______________________________

3. ______________________________

C. What are three advantages of using hydroelectricity?

1. ______________________________

2. ______________________________

3. ______________________________

Renewable Energy

In addition to hydroelectricity, there are several other sources of renewable energy used in North America. Two of the most important sources of renewable energy are the sun and the wind.

Solar Power

Solar power is energy that we get from the sun in the form of heat and light.

Solar Panels

Solar power that can be used to heat water is called *solar thermal power.* In North America, the most common use of solar thermal power is for heating swimming pools. The first solar thermal power plant was built in the Mojave Desert in 1984. Even though this project was a success, few solar thermal plants have been built since.

Solar power can also be used to create electrical energy. Solar panels collect light and turn it into electricity that can be used in homes and businesses. Large systems can even generate enough electricity to meet the needs of entire cities. However, although sunlight is free, ways of collecting and converting it to electricity are still very expensive, so there are not many large solar power plants in North America. Some of the largest solar plants are located in Ontario, Canada, and in Nevada and California in the U.S.

Wind Power

The same wind that lifts a kite into the air can also generate electricity for thousands of homes. People collect the power of the wind using *wind turbines.*

Wind Turbines

Wind turbines are huge towers with giant blades that are spun by the wind. The spinning turbines power generators that make electricity.

When many wind turbines are built together in one place, they are called a wind farm. Wind farms are built in places that get a lot of wind.

In North America, the vast majority of wind farms are found in the United States. However, there are some in Canada and Mexico as well.

The largest wind farm in the world has 627 turbines and is located in Texas. This wind farm makes enough electricity to power over 230,000 homes!

Renewable Energy

A. Find and circle the solar and wind power words in the word puzzle. Words may appear across, down, or diagonally.

E	C	O	L	L	E	C	T	B	V	H	T	H	E
N	G	N	M	O	Z	E	T	N	E	K	G	T	L
E	R	X	R	M	W	P	O	A	J	Y	E	U	E
R	S	P	E	C	O	N	V	E	R	T	M	R	C
G	W	I	N	D	F	A	R	M	W	Y	I	B	T
Y	H	R	E	I	M	A	T	A	S	Y	B	I	R
E	S	E	W	U	M	G	T	B	E	A	R	N	I
S	O	L	A	R	P	A	N	E	L	T	U	E	C
R	R	T	B	I	E	M	H	E	R	A	T	O	I
N	O	H	L	H	W	S	U	O	Y	O	D	H	T
D	Q	G	E	N	E	R	A	T	O	R	U	E	Y
E	G	E	H	T	E	T	U	C	O	S	Y	A	S

blades
collect
convert
electricity
energy
generator
heat
renewable
solar panel
turbine
wind farm

B. Choose three words from the word box and write a sentence using each word. Underline the words you used from the box.

1. ____

____

2. ____

____

3. ____

____

Fishing

Fishing is a big industry in the coastal areas of North America. Many people depend on fishing to earn a living. Canada, the sixth-largest exporter of fish in the world, brings in more than 2 billion dollars each year from selling fish. The United States is the world's third-largest seafood producer and, like Canada, also exports much of the fish it catches. Mexico also ranks in the top 20 seafood producers in the world.

The largest fishing zone in North America is in the North Atlantic Ocean. About 25% of the world's fish comes from this area, which stretches from Newfoundland in Canada to New England in the northeastern United States. Another large fishing area is located in the Pacific Ocean, along the coasts of California, Oregon, Washington, British Columbia, and Alaska.

People once thought the supply of fish was endless. But in recent years, there have been disturbing signs that many species of fish are declining. Wild salmon are just one example of a threatened species.

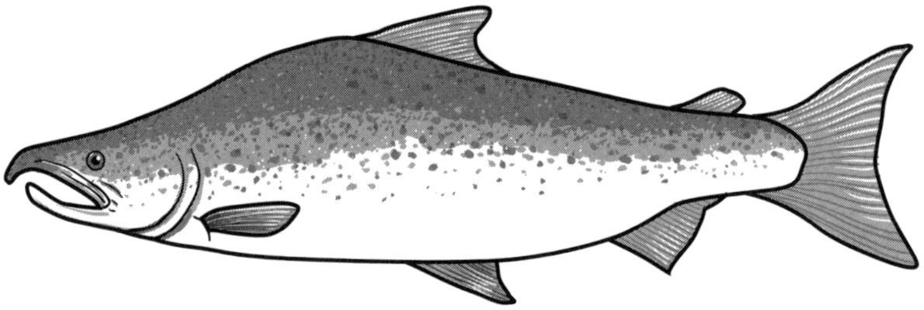

Wild Alaskan Sockeye Salmon

North American salmon live along the Pacific coast from Alaska to California. In the wild, salmon are born in freshwater streams and rivers. They make their way downstream to the ocean, where they spend most of their lives. When they are ready to breed, they swim upstream in order to return to the same place where they were *spawned*, or hatched. Over the last several decades, there has been a sharp decrease in the wild salmon population. Pollution, dams, overfishing, and other human activity have contributed to this decline.

In order to meet the demand for salmon as a food, the industry of salmon farming has grown. Farmed salmon live in large underwater cages in the ocean. These cages are usually made of mesh and framed by steel. Each cage can hold up to 90,000 fish and keep the fish safe from potential predators. However, there are concerns that farmed salmon are also contributing to the declining populations of wild salmon. Escaped farmed salmon can spread diseases and parasites to the wild salmon population. They can also breed with the wild salmon and reduce the chances of their offspring surviving.

Fishing

A. Look at the map. Circle the names of the seafood that you have eaten. Draw a star next to the one you liked best.

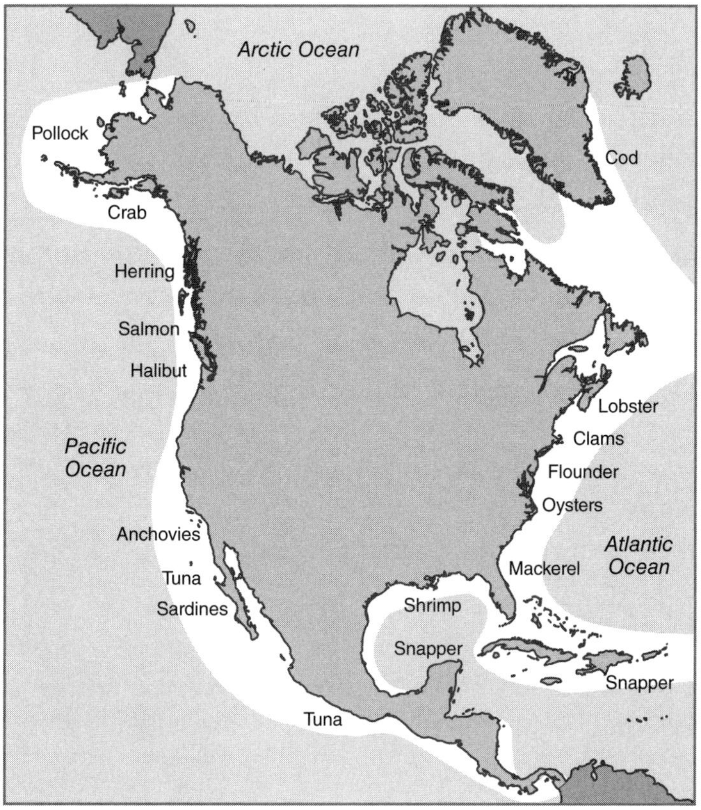

B. Use the information on the other page to help you answer the questions.

1. Where is the largest fishing zone in North America? ____________________

2. Which country is the sixth-largest exporter of fish? ____________________

3. What are three human activities that have contributed to the decline of wild salmon?

____

4. What negative effects have farmed salmon had on the wild salmon population?

____

____

Corn and Livestock

Although many kinds of crops are grown in North America, corn is one of the biggest. Most of the corn crop is used to feed livestock such as cattle. Cattle are the most common type of livestock in North America, and they are raised for both beef and milk.

Corn

In North America, corn is grown from the southern parts of Canada down to Mexico. The vast majority of corn crops are grown in the midwestern United States. The U.S. produces half the world's corn supply.

About 80% of the corn grown in the United States is used for animal feed. Another 12% is eaten by people. Some of this is in the form of fresh, canned, or frozen corn, and some is in products such as corn chips or tortillas.

Corn is also used to make a sweetener called high fructose corn syrup. High fructose corn syrup is used in many store-bought foods because it is inexpensive and helps the foods stay fresh longer. However, many doctors are concerned about the negative effects of high fructose corn syrup. Eating large amounts of it over a long period of time has been linked with gaining too much weight and developing diabetes, high blood pressure, and heart disease.

Corn is also used to make *ethanol*. Ethanol is a type of fuel that can be used to run cars. Unlike gasoline, ethanol is a renewable resource. However, it takes a great deal of processing to make ethanol, and it still causes pollution when it is used as fuel.

Livestock

Although cattle are raised in Canada, Mexico, and Central America, the majority of cattle are raised in the midwestern and southern regions of the United States. With about 95 million cattle, the United States produces more beef than any other country.

Most beef cattle are raised in feedlots. They are fed mostly corn for about 140 days, at which time they are ready for slaughter. About 40% of the beef produced in the U.S. comes from large feedlots with over 32,000 animals.

Cows are also raised for milk production. Dairy cows are raised in all 50 states of the U.S., but the top milk-producing states are California, Wisconsin, New York, and Idaho. Milk is also made into cheese, yogurt, butter, ice cream, and other dairy products.

The United States also raises more chickens and turkeys than any other country. In addition, the U.S. is a leading producer of eggs, with over 90 billion eggs produced each year!

Name ___________________________

Corn and Livestock

Use the information on the other page to crack the secret code. Read each clue below and write the correct word on the lines. Then use the numbers to crack the code!

1. The United States produces ____ of the world's supply of corn.

   ___ ___ ___ ___
   22 15 26 20

2. About 80% of the ____ grown in the United States is used to feed livestock.

   ___ ___ ___ ___
   17 3 6 2

3. Corn can be used to make a fuel source called ____.

   ___ ___ ___ ___ ___ ___ ___
   19 8 22 15 2 3 26

4. Most beef cattle are raised in ____.

   ___ ___ ___ ___ ___ ___ ___ ___
   20 19 19 18 26 3 8 7

5. The state of ____ is one of the top producers of dairy products.

   ___ ___ ___ ___ ___ ___ ___ ___ ___ ___
   17 15 26 23 20 3 6 2 23 15

6. The United States produces more chickens and ____ than any other country.

   ___ ___ ___ ___ ___ ___ ___
   8 9 6 25 19 13 7

Crack the Code!

____ are the most common breed of dairy cow in the United States because they produce the most milk.

___ ___ ___ ___ ___ ___ ___ ___ ___
22 3 26 7 8 19 23 2 7

Coffee and Bananas

Mexico and the seven countries of Central America grow a lot of coffee and bananas. In fact, Central America produces 10% of the world's supply of both bananas and coffee. Bananas are grown in the tropical lowlands, while coffee thrives in the highlands.

Banana Tree

Coffee Plant

Coffee and Banana Production in Mexico and Central America

Country	Tons of Bananas Per Year	Tons of Coffee Per Year
Belize	75,016	50
Costa Rica	2,074,311	118,232
El Salvador	71,650	107,726
Guatemala	1,730,034	280,869
Honduras	1,003,103	240,250
Mexico	1,964,545	268,865
Nicaragua	39,997	80,168
Panama	394,474	14,286

Food and Agriculture Organization of the United Nations

A. Use the information from the chart to answer the questions.

1. Together, the three largest banana producers grow about how many tons of bananas yearly?

   less than 1 million tons **almost 5 million tons** **over 5 million tons**

2. Together, the three largest coffee producers grow about how many tons of coffee yearly?

   over 8 million tons **nearly 800,000 tons** **less than 80,000 tons**

Name ______________________________

Coffee and Bananas

B. Circle the answer that completes each sentence. Use the chart on the other page to help you.

1. Mexico grows nearly 2 million tons of ____.	**coffee**	**bananas**
2. Coffee is grown in the ____.	**highlands**	**lowlands**
3. ____ produces the most bananas.	**Guatemala**	**Costa Rica**
4. ____ produces the most coffee.	**Guatemala**	**Costa Rica**
5. Honduras produces more ____.	**coffee**	**bananas**
6. El Salvador produces more ____.	**coffee**	**bananas**

C. Look at the map of Mexico and Central America below. Number the countries from **1** to **8** according to how many tons of bananas they produce each year.

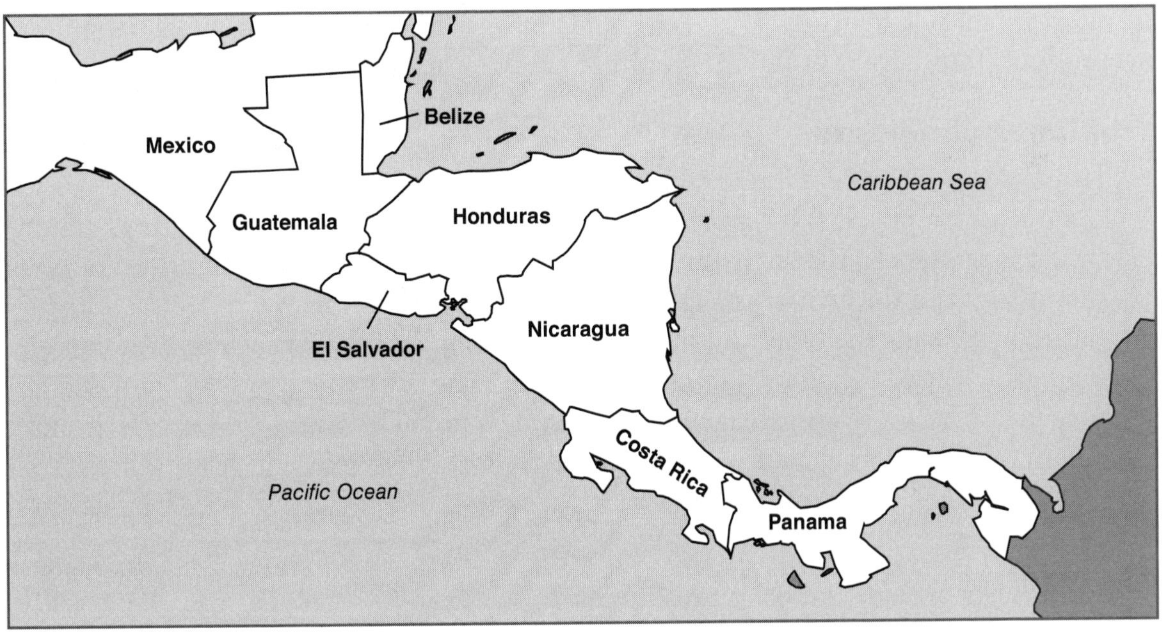

North America's Forests

Forests are an important natural resource in North America. They provide food and homes for many animals. They also provide the planet with oxygen. When forests are logged, trees can be made into products such as paper, furniture, and lumber.

Coniferous Forests

Coniferous forests cover most of Canada, as well as parts of the western United States. Coniferous trees have cones and needles for leaves. They do not lose their needles in the winter and, for this reason, are sometimes called *evergreens*. Types of coniferous trees include pine, spruce, cedar, and fir. Some of the tallest and oldest coniferous trees in the world are the redwoods in northern California. Coniferous forests are logged to produce lumber for buildings and for products such as toilet paper, cardboard, and printer paper. In Canada, most of the lumber is exported for use in the United States.

Deciduous Forests

Deciduous forests are found primarily in eastern North America. Deciduous trees have leaves that drop off in autumn. The deciduous trees in the New England region of the U.S. are known for their leaves turning beautiful shades of yellow, orange, brown, and red each fall. Some examples of deciduous trees are oak, maple, beech, chestnut, elm, and aspen. Wood from deciduous forests is used to make paper products, lumber for building, furniture, and musical instruments.

Tropical Rainforests

Tropical rainforests are found in Mexico, Central America, and on some of the Caribbean islands. It rains a great deal in a rainforest and is hot and humid. This climate creates a fertile environment. There are tens of thousands of different plants and animals in the rainforest. Trees are so crowded that they must compete for sunlight. Most of the trees and plants form a *canopy* over the rainforest. Some tall trees grow above the canopy to reach the light. The ones that grow below the canopy have broad leaves to absorb as much sunlight as possible. Vines, flowers, ferns, and other plants grow everywhere, even on the trees themselves. With over 900 different species of trees, the rainforests in Costa Rica are thought to be some of the world's most diverse.

Rainforests provide important resources. In addition to supplying the planet with oxygen, they are also full of plants that can be used to make medicines. Unfortunately, many of the rainforests are being cleared for lumber or to make room for grazing cattle and growing crops. Many rainforest plants and animals have lost their habitats and are endangered or already extinct.

North America's Forests

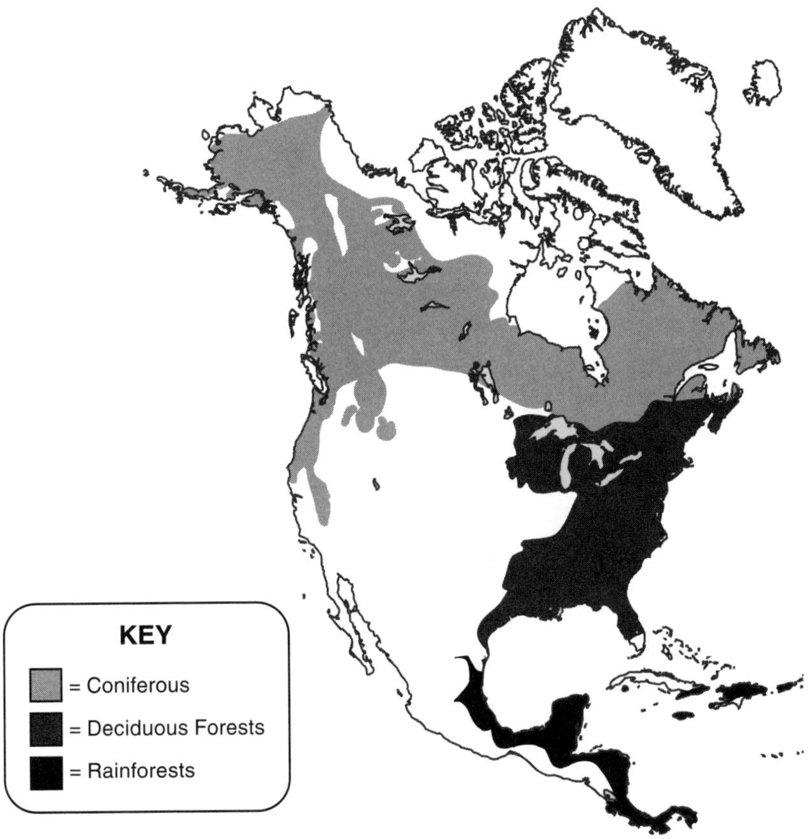

Unscramble the word below each line to complete the sentence. Use the information on the other page to help you.

1. Rainforests provide ____________________ to the planet.
   gonexy

2. Coniferous trees have cones and ____________________.
   selened

3. Deciduous trees lose their leaves in ____________________.
   tamunu

4. Examples of ____________________ trees are pine, cedar, and spruce.
   cfoisroneu

5. Plants found in rainforests can be used to make ____________________.
   dimecinse

6. The trees in ____________________ turn red, yellow, and orange.
   enw danglen

Wildlife of North America

Polar Bear

The polar bear is the world's largest land carnivore, or meat eater.

Habitat
- polar ice cap in the Arctic Circle

Characteristics
- male weighs up to 1,600 lbs (720 kg)
- black skin under white fur absorbs sunlight
- layer of fat keeps the bear warm

Diet
- mostly seals, which the bear sneaks up on by waiting near holes in the ice

Behavior
- hunts and lives alone
- excellent swimmer

Life Cycle
- mates in spring
- mother gives birth to two cubs in snow or ice dens in winter
- cubs live with the mother for several years
- lives 25 to 30 years in the wild

Status
- threatened due to global warming

Humpback Whale

The humpback whale is a baleen whale, meaning it filters food from the water.

Habitat
- migrates up to 31,000 miles (50,000 km) from the arctic regions in summer to warmer waters in winter

Characteristics
- up to 52 feet (16 m) in length
- black on top with white underbelly
- long, narrow flippers

Diet
- krill, which are small shrimp-like animals

Behavior
- travel in groups
- can jump completely out of the water

Life Cycle
- breeds in warm waters in winter
- mother gives birth to a single calf, which stays with its mother for a year
- lives for about 50 years in the wild

Status
- once endangered from overhunting; still considered a threatened species

Wildlife of North America

Bison

Although bison are often confused with buffalo, they are actually more closely related to cattle.

Habitat
- the Great Plains region of North America in both the U.S. and Canada

Characteristics
- shaggy, dark-brown fur; large heads; and short, curved horns
- adult male weighs up to 2,000 lbs (900 kg)

Diet
- mostly grass and herbs

Behavior
- live in small bands that often come together to form large herds
- migrate a few hundred miles south in winter

Life Cycle
- mate in August; males engage in fierce head-butting contests to win their mates
- females usually give birth to a single calf in May

Status
- once near extinction, there are over 450,000 bison today

Beaver

Beavers are the largest rodent in North America.

Habitat
- live in lodges they construct from tree branches in marshes, lakes, ponds, and small rivers

Characteristics
- large, strong teeth for gnawing through tree trunks and powerful, paddle-shaped tails for swimming
- thick waterproof fur

Diet
- the soft layer beneath the bark of trees, as well as leaves, twigs, and buds

Behavior
- build dams and lodges
- live in family groups inside the lodge

Life Cycle
- mate once a year and produce a litter of about four kits
- kits stay in the lodge for two years
- live about 20 years in the wild

Status
- people hunted beavers for their pelts and the species was almost extinct by 1900; has since recovered

Wildlife of North America

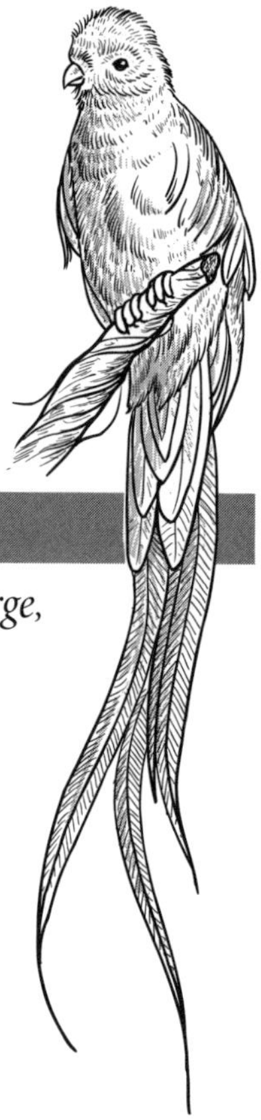

Gila Monster

The Gila monster is the only venomous lizard that is native to the United States.

Habitat
- lives in the Mojave, Sonoran, and Chihuahuan deserts in the United States and Mexico

Characteristics
- can reach up to 2 feet (60 cm) in length
- black with pink and yellow markings and black bands around its thick tail

Diet
- uses its venom to kill rats, mice, and other small mammals, as well as birds and lizards

Behavior
- lives in burrows it digs in the sand
- can go for months without food

Life Cycle
- female lays 3 to 15 eggs in a hole she digs in the sand
- baby Gilas are about 4 inches (10 cm) long
- lives for about 20 years

Status
- threatened by loss of habitat due to humans
- protected in the states of Nevada and Arizona

Quetzal

The name "quetzal" means "large, brilliant tail feather."

Habitat
- tropical rainforests of Central America

Characteristics
- brightly colored feathers in shades of green, red, and white
- male has tail feathers that are up to 3 feet (1 m) long

Diet
- fruit, worms, frogs, and insects

Behavior
- poor flyer
- avoids predators such as gray squirrels, hawks, and owls by blending in with its environment

Life Cycle
- makes nests in rotted tree stumps
- female lays two or three light-blue eggs
- both parents care for the hatchlings that fly at about three weeks old

Status
- endangered due to habitat loss and hunting of their unique feathers
- do not survive in captivity

Wildlife of North America

A. Circle the name of the animal that completes each sentence.

1. ____ live in the deserts of the United States and Mexico.

   quetzals **bison** **Gila monsters**

2. The ____ is the largest land carnivore.

   polar bear **bison** **quetzal**

3. The ____ has babies that are called kits.

   quetzal **beaver** **humpback whale**

4. The ____ is a venomous carnivore.

   polar bear **Gila monster** **humpback whale**

5. The ____ migrates over 30,000 miles each year.

   humpback whale **quetzal** **bison**

6. The ____ eats mostly seals.

   Gila monster **polar bear** **humpback whale**

7. ____ live in the rainforests of Central America.

   quetzals **Gila monsters** **beavers**

8. The ____ eats mostly krill.

   bison **Gila monster** **humpback whale**

9. ____ are grazing animals.

   bison **beavers** **polar bears**

10. ____ live together in family groups inside lodges.

    Gila monsters **beavers** **quetzals**

B. Which of the six animals is your favorite? Why?

____

Review

Use words from the box to complete the crossword puzzle.

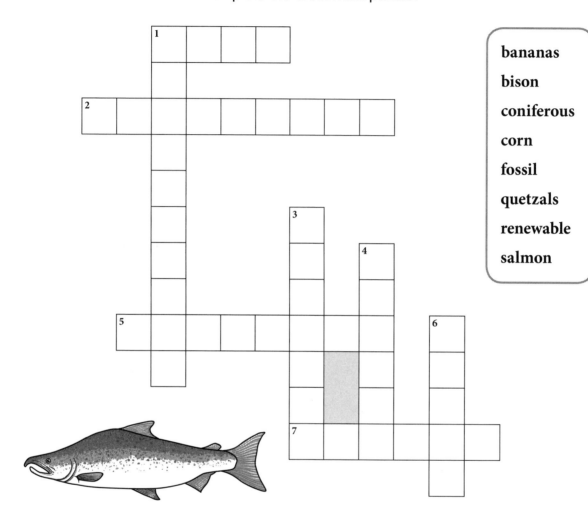

bananas
bison
coniferous
corn
fossil
quetzals
renewable
salmon

Across

1. Most of the U.S.'s _____ crop is used to feed livestock.
2. Wind is a _____ resource.
5. _____ live in the Central American rainforest.
7. Today, most _____ are farmed rather than caught in the wild.

Down

1. _____ forests cover most of Canada.
3. Mexico grows nearly 2 million tons of _____ each year.
4. Oil, natural gas, and coal are _____ fuels.
6. _____ live mostly in the Great Plains region of North America.

SECTION 5

North American Culture

This section introduces students to the beliefs and traditions of North American people. Students learn about cultural influences such as music, art, and sports that are important aspects of life in North America. They also learn about different types of North American cuisine and celebrations, as well as religions and native cultures.

Each skill in this section is based on the following National Geography Standards:

Essential Element 2: Places and Regions

Standard 6: How culture and experience influence people's perceptions of places and regions

Essential Element 4: Human Systems

Standard 10: The characteristics, distribution, and complexity of Earth's cultural mosaics

CONTENTS

Overview

The culture of a group of people is reflected in its customs, traditions, and beliefs. One way to learn about a particular culture is to explore its history, celebrations, art, and literature. Just as the land of North America is quite diverse, the culture of the continent differs vastly from region to region.

Tourist Attractions

One of the most famous tourist attractions in North America is the Statue of Liberty National Monument in New York Harbor, which includes the Statue of Liberty and Ellis Island, where visitors can learn about immigrants who came to the U.S. In Mexico, visitors marvel at the ancient Mayan ruins of Chichén Itzá. To the north, tourists can learn about Canadian history at the fortifications, or military buildings, of Quebec.

Arts and Entertainment

Many styles of music, including mariachi, reggae, and jazz, began in North America. Many famous artists come from North America, as well as some of the world's most loved and respected authors. Another popular form of entertainment in North America is playing or watching sports such as soccer or baseball.

Major Religions

Although the majority of people in North America are Christian, many other religions are observed. Many people come to North America to practice their religion without fear of cruel treatment because of their beliefs.

Native Cultures

Many groups of people are native to North America. This means that before any Europeans reached the continent, people were already living there. Native cultures in North America include the Inuit people of Canada, the Tarahumara tribe in Mexico, and the Cherokee people in the United States.

Cuisine

Immigrants who came to North America brought their favorite recipes and cooking methods with them. This has resulted in a wide variety of foods in the United States and Canada. In Mexico and Central America, many dishes include foods such as corn, beans, tomatoes, and rice, which were introduced by the Spanish in the 1500s.

Celebrations

In many countries throughout North America, including the United States, Independence Day is an important national holiday. In Mexico, the Day of the Dead is a special holiday to honor those who have passed away.

Overview

Fill in the bubble to answer each question.

1. Which of these is *not* a style of music that started in North America?

   Ⓐ jazz

   Ⓑ polka

   Ⓒ reggae

   Ⓓ mariachi

2. Which of these is *not* a native culture of North America?

   Ⓐ the Tarahumara

   Ⓑ the Cherokee

   Ⓒ the Inuit

   Ⓓ the Irish

3. Which of these is the major religion of North America?

   Ⓐ Islam

   Ⓑ Buddhism

   Ⓒ Judaism

   Ⓓ Christianity

4. In which country is the Day of the Dead celebrated?

   Ⓐ Mexico

   Ⓑ the Bahamas

   Ⓒ Canada

   Ⓓ Costa Rica

5. Which of these tourist attractions was *not* mentioned as being in North America?

   Ⓐ Fortifications of Quebec

   Ⓑ Chichén Itzá

   Ⓒ Big Ben

   Ⓓ Ellis Island

Tourist Attractions

There are many interesting landmarks to visit in North America. These sites attract millions of tourists each year who want to learn more about North America's history and culture.

Statue of Liberty and Ellis Island

Ellis Island

The Statue of Liberty National Monument is located in New York Harbor, close to both New York City and the state of New Jersey. Visitors come from all over the world to see the famous statue and to visit nearby Ellis Island. Ellis Island is important to the history of the United States. From 1892 to 1954, Ellis Island was the first stop for over 12 million immigrants who wanted to start a new life in the U.S. As their ships entered the harbor, the new residents saw the Statue of Liberty raising her lamp in welcome. The famous statue, nicknamed Lady Liberty, was a gift from France.

Chichén Itzá

The ruins of the ancient city of Chichén Itzá are located in the Mexican state of Yucatán. The city was first built by the Mayans in the 6th century. Perhaps the most impressive building in the city is El Castillo (The Castle), a 79-foot-tall pyramid. There are 365 steps on the pyramid, the same as the number of days in a year. Twice a year, on the spring and autumn equinoxes, a shadow cast by the setting sun looks like a snake moving down the stairs. Another fascinating structure of Chichén Itzá is a large court made for playing an ancient game called *tlachtli*. Some researchers believe that losing the game cost the players their lives. The court walls are decorated with sculptures of the winners holding the severed heads of the losers.

Fortifications of Quebec

The city of Quebec in Canada is home to a variety of military structures, including a 2.9 mile (4.6 km) wall that surrounds part of the city. The fortifications include towers, guard posts, living quarters, and the Citadel. The Citadel was a command center and a stronghold to protect the people in the event of an attack. Thousands of people come to visit the fortifications every year. They can explore ancient-looking towers and turrets. There are also old cannons mounted along the walls, as well as information about how the fortifications were built and used.

Tourist Attractions

A. Unscramble the word below each line to complete the sentence. Use the information on the other page to help you.

1. ______________________ is located in New York Harbor.
   slile dinals

2. Over 12 million ______________________ came to Ellis Island.
   ramimsting

3. Ellis Island is now part of the Statue of Liberty National ______________________.
   netommun

4. The ruins of Chichén Itzá are in the country of ______________________.
   cimoxe

5. Chichén Itzá was founded by the ______________________.
   anamsy

6. El Castillo was built in the shape of a ______________________.
   maydrip

7. El Castillo has 365 ______________________.
   pesst

8. There is a ______________________ for playing tlachtli at Chichén Itzá.
   rutoc

9. The ______________________ was a command center in Quebec.
   tadelic

10. The visitors of the Quebec fortifications can explore ______________________.
    retrust

B. Which of the three places on the other page would you like to visit the most? Why? Explain your answer.

____

____

____

Arts and Entertainment

Visual Arts

Artist	Fast Facts
Ansel Adams 1902–1984	• American photographer known for his black and white photos of nature in the western United States, especially Yosemite National Park
Margaret Bourke-White 1904–1971	• American photographer and photojournalist • first female war correspondent allowed to work in combat zones during World War II
Alexander Calder 1898–1976	• American sculptor who invented the mobile (moving sculpture) • created a miniature mechanical circus
Frida Kahlo 1907–1954	• Mexican painter best known for her bold, brightly colored self-portraits • married to famous Mexican artist Diego Rivera
Georgia O'Keeffe 1887–1986	• American artist known for her paintings of flowers, bones, rocks, and shells • painted landscapes of the southwestern United States
Diego Rivera 1886–1957	• Mexican painter famous for his large outdoor murals that often showed historical or political scenes • married to famous Mexican artist Frida Kahlo
Andy Warhol 1928–1987	• American artist who painted realistic images of products such as Campbells® soup cans and Coca-Cola® bottles • painted portraits of celebrities in bright colors

Write the letter of the clue that describes each artist.

____ 1. Ansel Adams

____ 2. Alexander Calder

____ 3. Frida Kahlo

____ 4. Georgia O'Keeffe

____ 5. Margaret Bourke-White

____ 6. Andy Warhol

____ 7. Diego Rivera

a. painted bold self-portraits

b. photographed combat zones

c. invented the mobile

d. painted pictures of soup cans

e. painted historical and political murals

f. photographed natural places

g. painted flowers, bones, shells, and rocks

Name ______________________________

Arts and Entertainment

Totem Poles

Totem poles are an artform developed by Native Americans on the Pacific coast of the United States and Canada. A totem pole is created by carving figures into a large cedar tree trunk. The figures are usually painted black, white, red, green, green-blue, and yellow.

Together, the figures on the totem pole tell a story. The story could be a legend, the history of a family, or a depiction of an important event. In the past, a family member would interpret the symbols on the pole to tell the story.

Poles were also carved to ridicule or shame a person. If a person did not repay a debt, his or her image might be carved upside down on one of the poles and displayed for everyone to see. However, in most cases, totem poles were carved for more positive reasons, such as welcoming visitors or marking the grave of an important person.

Some Native American artists still make totem poles today. They follow traditional methods and do not use modern tools such as chain saws or electric drills.

Color the totem pole in the traditional Native American colors mentioned above. Then complete the caption below.

I think this totem pole tells a story about ______________________________

____.

Arts and Entertainment

Music

Many different types of music are played throughout North America. Some forms of popular music originated on the continent.

Mariachi

Mariachi is a style of Mexican music that began in the late 1700s. A traditional Mariachi band consisted of musicians playing the guitar, the *vihuela* (a guitar with six sets of double strings), and the *guitarrón* (a large bass guitar). Violins, trumpets, and singers were added in later years. Mariachi musicians wear matching suits and large hats called *sombreros.*

Reggae

Reggae got its start in Jamaica in the 1960s and became popular throughout the world. Reggae is a blend of traditional African sounds and rock and roll. Song lyrics usually focus on feelings of social injustice and the challenges of living in poverty. Reggae's most well-known artist is Bob Marley. His music is still popular today.

Bob Marley

Jazz

Jazz got its start in the early 1900s in the southern U.S. Popular jazz instruments include the trumpet, trombone, bass, piano, and saxophone. Over the years, jazz has evolved into many styles, including cool jazz, bebop, and jazz fusion. Legendary jazz musicians include Duke Ellington and Miles Davis.

Miles Davis

Circle **yes** if the statement is true or **no** if it is false.

1. Mariachi is a kind of Mexican instrument. **Yes** **No**
2. A vihuela is a type of guitar. **Yes** **No**
3. Reggae began in Cuba. **Yes** **No**
4. Reggae is only popular in the Caribbean. **Yes** **No**
5. Bebop, jazz fusion, and cool jazz are all styles of jazz music. **Yes** **No**

Name ____________________

Arts and Entertainment

Literature

North America has produced many famous writers. Even though authors Laura Ingalls Wilder and Maya Angelou were born in different centuries, they both used personal experiences of growing up in North America to write their best-selling books.

Laura Ingalls Wilder

Laura Ingalls Wilder was born in Wisconsin in 1867. She and her family were pioneers in the midwestern United States. While she was still a little girl, Laura's family traveled by covered wagon to Kansas, where they lived for a few years before moving to Minnesota and then the Dakota territory. At age 15, Ingalls became a school teacher and taught in a one-room school. She married Almanzo Wilder a few years later.

Later in life, Ingalls began writing about her life as a pioneer in a series of books commonly known as the *Little House* books. The *Little House* books were very popular and are still read by children today. In addition, the books inspired a popular television show about the Ingalls family and life on the prairie.

Maya Angelou

Maya Angelou was born in 1928 in St. Louis, Missouri. She spent her early years with her grandmother in the small town of Stamps, Arkansas. The southern states practiced segregation at that time, and Angelou, an African-American, experienced racial discrimination firsthand. But in Stamps, she also experienced the values of faith, family, and community, and she learned to love the arts.

At different times in her life, Angelou has been a dancer, singer, actress, and teacher of music and drama. But she is best known for her six books that tell of her childhood and early adulthood experiences. The first of these books, *I Know Why the Caged Bird Sings*, is the most famous. It was made into a television movie in 1979. Angelou is also an acclaimed poet. She was asked by President Bill Clinton to compose and read a poem at his inauguration in 1993.

Name two ways that Maya Angelou and Laura Ingalls Wilder are the same. Then name two ways they are different.

Same: ____________________

____

Different: ____________________

____

Arts and Entertainment

Sports

Sports are a big part of life for many people in North America. Children often play on sports teams in their schools or communities. People also watch professional sports.

Football and Baseball

American football grew out of the English game of rugby. As rules and teams were established, football quickly gained popularity in the United States. Today, most high schools and colleges in the U.S. have football teams. Many people also watch professional football. The 2010 Super Bowl was viewed by over 100 million fans! However, American football is not nearly as popular in other parts of the world.

Baseball is another popular sport in the United States. Although variations of the game have been played for hundreds of years, the first official game was held in 1846 in Hoboken, New Jersey. Within 10 years of the first game, baseball was already being called "America's national pastime." Baseball is now a major sport in other parts of North America as well, including Canada, Cuba, Puerto Rico, the Dominican Republic, and Mexico.

Ice Hockey

Ice hockey is the most popular sport in Canada. Most big cities have ice rinks and professional hockey teams. Every year, Canadian and U.S. teams of the National Hockey League compete for the Stanley Cup.

Canada's greatest hockey star is Wayne Gretzky, who started his professional career at the age of 17. He was the youngest player ever to enter the National Hockey League. Gretzky played with the Edmonton Oilers for nine years, leading them to four Stanley Cup victories. He outscored every other player and won numerous awards. Gretzky retired from the sport in 1999 and was inducted into the Hockey Hall of Fame that same year.

Soccer

Soccer—called football in most countries outside the United States—is popular in Mexico and Central America. Soccer had its official start in Mexico on December 9, 1926. Since then, soccer has grown in popularity throughout the world. Many children and adults play in soccer leagues and enjoy watching professional matches. Mexico has hosted the World Cup soccer championship two times.

Arts and Entertainment

Sports

Using information from the other page, read each clue below and write the correct word on the lines. Then use the numbers to crack the code!

1. Hockey teams in Canada and the United States compete for the ____.

   24 25 6 19 17 10 4   8 26 21

2. The first official baseball game in the United States was held in ____, New Jersey.

   13 20 7 20 16 10 19

3. Wayne Gretzky played hockey for the ____ Oilers.

   10 9 18 20 19 25 20 19

4. Soccer is a popular sport in ____ and Central America.

   18 10 3 14 8 20

5. Over 100 million people watched the 2010 ____.

   24 26 21 10 23   7 20 2 17

6. Ice hockey is the most popular sport in ____.

   8 6 19 6 9 6

7. Mexico has hosted the ____ soccer championship two times.

   2 20 23 17 9   8 26 21

Crack the Code!

The ____ have won more World Series baseball championships than any other team.

19 10 2   4 20 23 16   4 6 19 16 10 10 24

Religions of North America

Christianity

Catholic Church

Although many religions are practiced in North America, about 86% of the people on the continent are Christian. Most Christians are either Roman Catholic or Protestant. The Protestant faith includes groups such as Methodist, Baptist, Lutheran, Amish, and Presbyterian. Other Christian religions include Mormonism and Jehovah's Witness.

People with the same religious beliefs often live in the same area. For example, most of the people who live in Mexico and Central America are Roman Catholic because when Spanish missionaries first came to these countries, they converted many of the native people to Catholicism. There are also many Roman Catholics in northeastern North America because many Catholic immigrants from Ireland and Italy settled there.

Many religious Christians live in what is frequently called the *Bible Belt* region of the United States. This region stretches across a number of southern and midwestern states. Many of these people belong to Baptist churches.

Two unique Christian groups are the Mormons and the Amish. In Utah, 77% of the people are members of the Church of Jesus Christ of Latter-Day Saints, also known as Mormons. In Pennsylvania, the Amish avoid technology, such as cars or computers, and are known for their plain clothing and skilled furniture making.

Circle the answer that completes each sentence. Use the information above to help you.

1. A person who is ____ is a Protestant.	**Lutheran**	**Catholic**
2. Most Mexicans are ____.	**Methodist**	**Catholic**
3. In Mexico, ____ missionaries converted many people to Catholicism.	**French**	**Spanish**
4. Catholics from ____ settled in the northeast.	**England**	**Ireland**
5. Many ____ live in the Bible Belt.	**Baptists**	**Amish**
6. About 77% of the population of Utah is ____.	**Presbyterian**	**Mormon**
7. Many ____ live in Pennsylvania.	**Mormons**	**Amish**

Name ____________________

Religions of North America

Other Religions

In addition to Christianity, several other religions are practiced in North America. These religions include Judaism, Islam, Buddhism, Hinduism, and traditional Native American religions. Together, these religions make up about 7% of the population. Just as with Christians, members of these religious groups tend to live in certain areas. For example, 75% of the Jews in Canada live in Toronto and Montreal. In the United States, many Jewish people live in New York and New Jersey. Across northern Canada and Alaska, native people practice the Inuit religion.

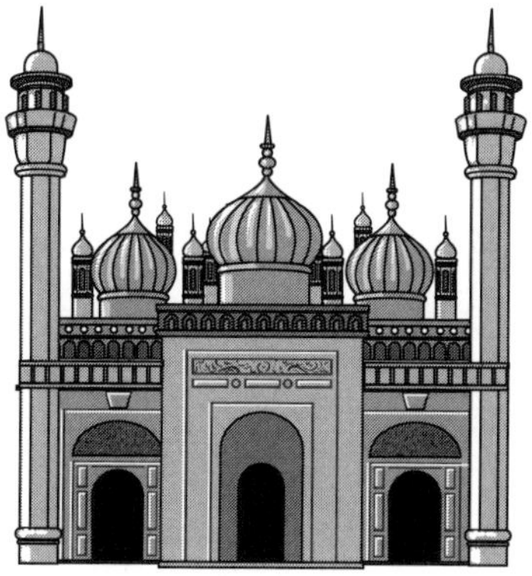

Muslim Mosque

Although Muslims—people who practice Islam—make up a very small percentage of the population, their numbers are growing. Some of this growth is due to Muslim immigrants coming to North America, and some is due to people who already live in North America converting to Islam.

About 6% of North America's population does not practice any specific religion. This group is also growing. Many young adults report that they are not a part of any religious group.

Use the information above to answer the questions.

1. Name four religions other than Christianity that are practiced in North America.

   ____________________ ____________________

   ____________________ ____________________

2. In what two cities do most of the Jewish people in Canada live?

   ____

3. What are two reasons the Muslim population is increasing in North America?

   ____

   ____

Native Cultures

Inuit

The Inuit are a people who originally lived in Alaska and gradually spread throughout the Arctic regions of Canada and Greenland. Because very little vegetation grows in this harsh climate, the traditional Inuit diet consisted almost entirely of meat. The Inuit hunted seals, walrus, caribou, musk oxen, and even polar bears. They used the animal hides to make warm clothing and boots called *mukluks*. They also used animal bones and tusks to make tools, hunting weapons, and small sculptures. Another animal that became important to the Inuit people was the husky, a dog used to pull sleds over the snow.

The Inuit language is still spoken, and many of the old traditions of hunting and traveling by sled remain. However, the culture has changed because of the influence of modern society. Most Inuit people hold jobs rather than living off the land. And Inuit children are educated in government schools.

Cherokee

The Cherokee are a group of Native American tribes that once lived in the southeastern United States. Cherokee villages were usually built near a river and included small, mud-plastered cabins and a large council house for meetings. The Cherokee farmed crops that included corn, beans, and squash. They also hunted deer, elk, and bear for both food and clothing. In the 1800s, the Cherokee developed their own written language and government, called the Cherokee Nation, modeled after the United States government.

In the winter of 1938, the American government forced the Cherokee people to leave their lands and move to land set aside for them in Oklahoma. Today, the Cherokee Nation is a thriving community, blending the old traditions with modern life.

Tarahumara

The Tarahumara live in the Copper Canyon region of northern Mexico. Most still live a traditional lifestyle that does not include modern technology. They live in caves, near cliffs, or in stone or log cabins. They eat a mostly vegetarian diet, growing their own corn, potatoes, squash, and beans. They also tend orchards of apples, peaches, papayas, and oranges.

The Tarahumara are known throughout the world for their amazing running ability. Villages in Copper Canyon are many miles apart, and the terrain is tough for vehicles or even horses, so foot travel is the only means of transportation. Both men and women can run extremely long distances without getting tired. In fact, they often run 50 to 80 miles every day! The Tarahumara hunt by simply chasing an animal until it gets too tired to run anymore. They do not wear any special shoes to run. Most run in sandals made from old tires and leather straps.

Name ______________________

Native Cultures

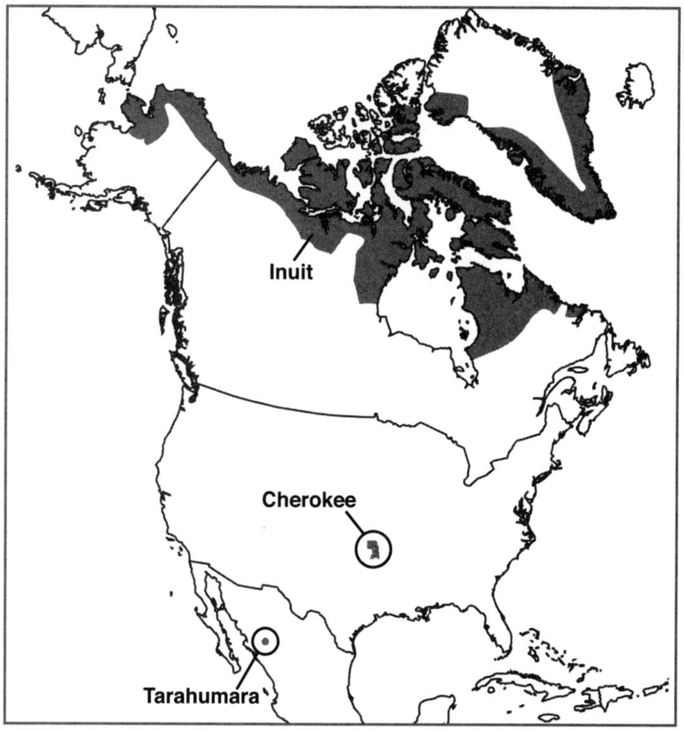

Use the information about the Inuit, the Cherokee, and the Tarahumara on the other page to write two interesting facts about each culture.

Inuit

1. ______________________

2. ______________________

Cherokee

1. ______________________

2. ______________________

Tarahumara

1. ______________________

2. ______________________

North American Cuisine

Mexican Cuisine

Mexican cuisine is a combination of traditional native foods and foods that were brought from Spain by early settlers.

In Mexico, corn has been a staple food for thousands of years. Corn is used to make tortillas, which are a part of many traditional Mexican foods such as tacos, enchiladas, and tostadas.

Other staple foods are rice, beans, and chili peppers. Rice is often served as a side dish. Beans are often mashed and refried to become part of the main dish or served on the side. Chili peppers are added to make foods spicy. The most popular pepper is the jalapeño, which is used in many traditional dishes. Chopped up chilies, onions, and tomatoes are mixed with spices to make salsa, a sauce that accompanies most Mexican meals.

Chocolate is also used in a wide variety of Mexican foods, from sweet to spicy. In fact, chocolate is a main ingredient in mole (MOH-lay), a sauce that is typically served over chicken.

Caribbean Cuisine

Caribbean cuisine contains a blend of several different cultures, including French, Spanish, Indian, African, and American. This is because people from so many parts of the world have settled on the islands.

Caribbean dishes often feature the fruits and vegetables native to the tropical climate, such as mangos, bananas, papayas, and avocados.

Goat meat is popular on many of the islands. It is frequently made into a stew with dumplings. Another popular dish is called *pelau* or "cook-up." To make this dish, the cook uses whatever meats and vegetables are on hand. Pelau is often served with rice or beans. Jerk seasoning is native to Jamaica and popular throughout the Caribbean. Typically, chicken or pork is dry-rubbed with a spice mixture that includes allspice—a type of dried fruit—and a very hot type of pepper.

Seafood is another popular choice in the Caribbean. All kinds of fish are eaten, including shark, crab, lobster, and conch (KONK), a type of shellfish. In the Bahamas, conch fritters are a favorite.

North American Cuisine

A. Find and circle the words in the word search. Words may appear across, down, or diagonally.

A	B	T	Y	K	H	S	G	T	I	P	A	J	M
D	F	S	V	A	E	B	X	O	G	E	U	O	P
C	P	C	L	E	U	G	N	S	G	L	B	U	D
D	B	H	C	Z	C	H	I	T	H	A	A	E	E
G	E	I	G	A	M	L	S	A	B	U	E	N	I
Z	R	L	C	O	C	A	M	D	E	E	P	C	O
Q	I	I	N	O	S	H	A	A	P	A	O	H	R
U	W	E	E	L	T	R	E	X	P	G	V	I	E
B	K	S	A	E	I	C	Q	L	N	M	E	L	T
S	N	S	E	B	T	O	P	A	P	A	Y	A	I
R	A	P	D	Z	N	N	M	A	A	E	V	D	T
Y	C	T	H	R	E	C	W	T	A	S	J	A	U
J	P	O	A	I	N	H	B	E	A	N	S	V	K
W	O	C	R	C	A	B	A	N	A	N	A	T	L
A	M	S	E	N	R	Z	L	P	O	W	O	T	Y

- banana
- beans
- chilies
- conch
- corn
- enchilada
- mango
- papaya
- pelau
- rice
- salsa
- tostada

B. In the word box, circle the names of the foods that you have eaten. Then write a sentence about Mexican food and a sentence about Caribbean food.

Mexican food: ____

____

Caribbean food: ____

____

Celebrations

Independence Day

Many countries in North America were once ruled by other countries. They celebrate their independence from those countries in different ways. For example, the United States was ruled by Great Britain and declared its independence on July 4, 1776. The U.S. celebrates its Independence Day with picnics, parades, and fireworks. The chart below gives information about other Independence Day celebrations.

Countries	Date	Commemorating Independence From...	Ways of Celebrating
Guatemala El Salvador Honduras Nicaragua Costa Rica	Sept. 15	Spain in 1821	To commemorate how the news of independence traveled from Guatemala to Costa Rica, a torch is carried through the five countries, arriving in Costa Rica on the eve of Independence Day. Other celebrations include a paper lantern parade, music, and parties.
Haiti	Jan. 1	France in 1804	Haitians eat a special pumpkin soup on Independence Day, which is also New Year's Day. When French colonists enslaved the local population, they would not allow the slaves to eat soup on special occasions. For the Haitian people, eating soup symbolizes freedom.
Bahamas	Jul. 10	Great Britain in 1973	People in the Bahamas celebrate the American Fourth of July as well as their own Independence Day, making a weeklong celebration of parties, picnics, and music. The final day ends in a special parade called a *junkanoo*, which features traditional music and elaborate costumes.

Use the information above to help you answer the questions.

1. From what country did Haiti declare independence? ____________________

2. On what date does Costa Rica celebrate its independence? ____________________

3. What is a junkanoo?

____

4. Why do people in Haiti eat soup on Independence Day?

____

Celebrations

Day of the Dead

The Day of the Dead is celebrated in Mexico on November 1 and 2. On these days, people remember and honor their ancestors, relatives, and friends who have passed away. Although it might seem that this would be a sad or scary holiday, it is actually a joyous one.

During the Day of the Dead, people visit cemeteries. Graves are cleaned up and decorated with flowers and gifts, including photos, favorite foods, and meaningful objects. People often have picnics in the cemetery and, in some parts of Mexico, spend the entire night at the graves of their loved ones. Many people also create shrines in their homes or businesses. These shrines are elaborately decorated with colorful banners; religious items such as crosses and statues of the Virgin Mary; and flowers, candles, food, and photos.

During this time, markets are full of toys and candies made in the shape of skeletons and skulls. People eat sugar skeletons and a special kind of bread called *Pan de Muertos* (Bread of the Dead), which is often shaped as a bun with two "bones," or long, thin pieces of bread, crossed over the top of it.

Use the information above to complete the paragraph about the Day of the Dead.

People in ____________________ celebrate the Day of the Dead on the first two days of the month of ____________________. On these days, people remember those who have died. A common activity is to visit ____________________ to clean up and decorate grave sites. People also bring food to have ____________________ in the cemetery and sometimes spend the entire night there. In addition, people create decorative ____________________ in their homes to honor the dead. During the Day of the Dead celebration, people can buy candies and toys made in the shape of skulls and ____________________. People eat a special kind of bread called ____________________, which means "Bread of the Dead" in Spanish.

Review

Use words from the box to complete the crossword puzzle.

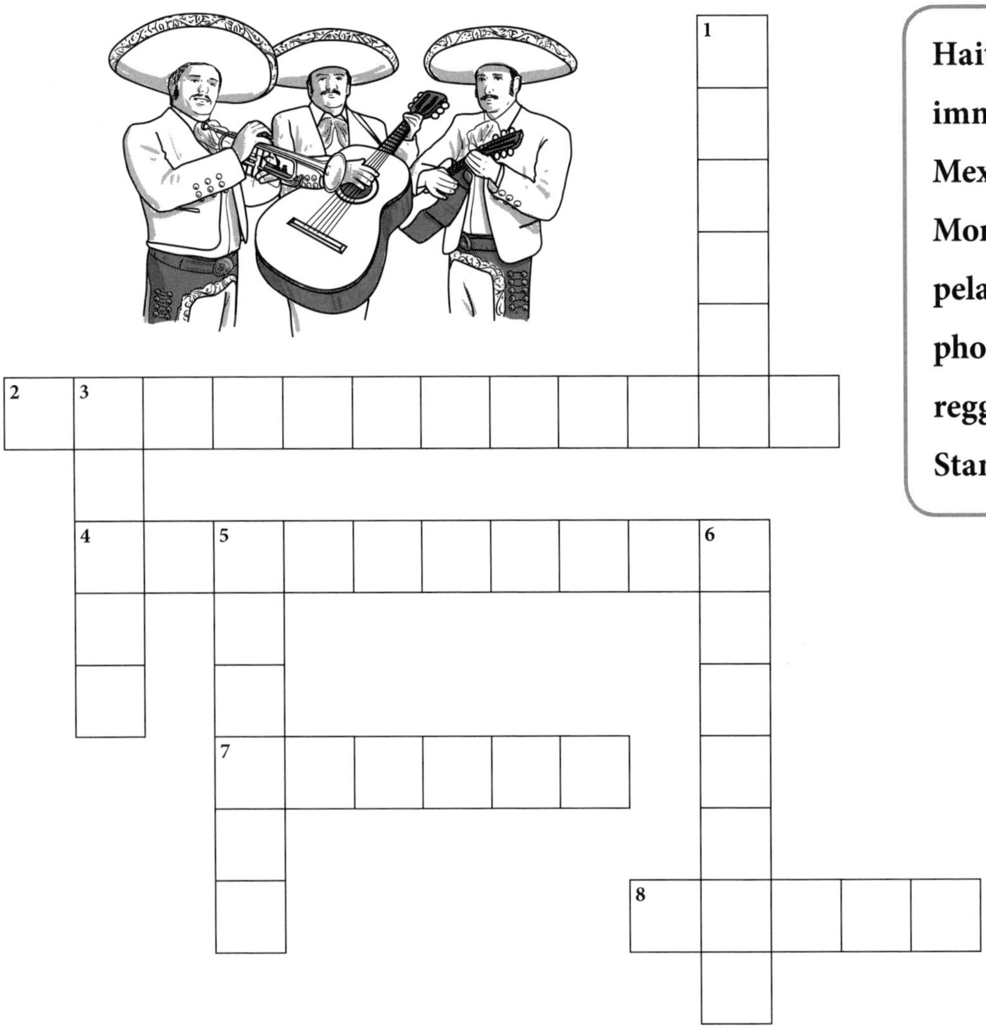

Haiti
immigrants
Mexico
Mormon
pelau
photographer
reggae
Stanley

Across

2. Ansel Adams was a famous ____.
4. Many ____ came to the United States by way of Ellis Island.
7. The Day of the Dead is celebrated in ____.
8. ____ is a traditional dish in the Caribbean.

Down

1. ____ is a kind of music that started in Jamaica in the 1960s.
3. People in ____ eat a special kind of soup on Independence Day.
5. Most of the population of Utah is ____.
6. Hockey players in Canada and the U.S. compete for the ____ Cup.

SECTION 6

Assessment

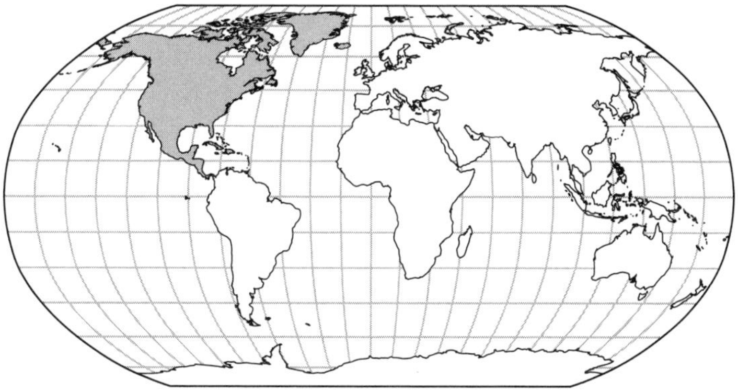

This section provides two cumulative assessments that you can use to evaluate students' acquisition of the information presented in this book. The first assessment requires students to identify selected cities, countries, landforms, and bodies of water on a combined physical and political map. The second assessment is a two-page multiple-choice test covering information from all sections of the book. Use one or both assessments as culminating activities for your class's study of North America.

CONTENTS

Name ______________________

Map Test

Write the name of the country, city, landform, river, or ocean that matches each number. Use the words in the box to help you.

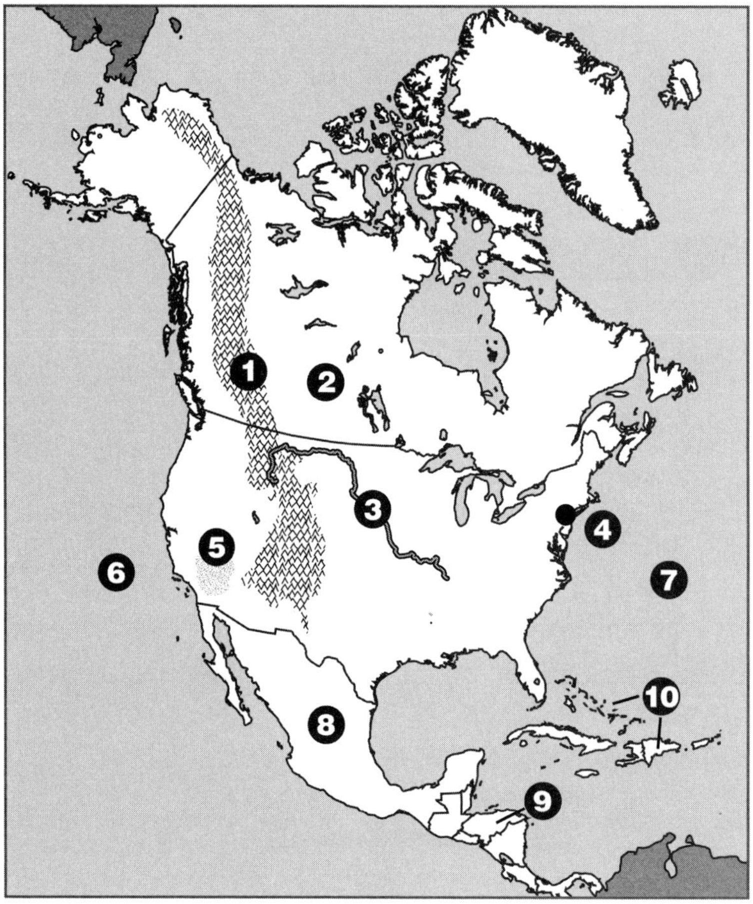

Mexico	Missouri River	New York City	Pacific Ocean	Rocky Mountains
Canada	Honduras	Atlantic Ocean	Mojave Desert	Caribbean Islands

1. ______________________
2. ______________________
3. ______________________
4. ______________________
5. ______________________
6. ______________________
7. ______________________
8. ______________________
9. ______________________
10. ______________________

Multiple-Choice Test

Fill in the bubble to answer each question or complete each sentence.

1. North America is the ____-largest continent in area.
   - Ⓐ second
   - Ⓑ third
   - Ⓒ fourth
   - Ⓓ fifth

2. Which ocean is east of North America?
   - Ⓐ Atlantic
   - Ⓑ Arctic
   - Ⓒ Pacific
   - Ⓓ Indian

3. In which two hemispheres is North America located?
   - Ⓐ Northern and Southern
   - Ⓑ Eastern and Western
   - Ⓒ Southern and Western
   - Ⓓ Northern and Western

4. Which of these is *not* a country in Central America?
   - Ⓐ Jamaica
   - Ⓑ Costa Rica
   - Ⓒ Belize
   - Ⓓ Guatemala

5. Which one is the tallest mountain in the Rocky Mountain range?
   - Ⓐ Mount Elbert
   - Ⓑ Blanca Peak
   - Ⓒ Mount St. Helens
   - Ⓓ Mount Massive

6. In which two countries are the four major deserts of North America located?
   - Ⓐ United States and Canada
   - Ⓑ Mexico and Panama
   - Ⓒ United States and Mexico
   - Ⓓ United States and Haiti

7. Which of these is *not* one of the Great Lakes?
   - Ⓐ Lake Michigan
   - Ⓑ Lake Erie
   - Ⓒ Lake Ohio
   - Ⓓ Lake Superior

8. Which one is the longest river in North America?
   - Ⓐ Mississippi
   - Ⓑ Missouri
   - Ⓒ Colorado
   - Ⓓ Yukon

Multiple-Choice Test

9. Which of these is *not* a renewable resource?
   - Ⓐ wind
   - Ⓑ solar power
   - Ⓒ natural gas
   - Ⓓ hydropower

10. Most of the corn grown in North America is used to ____.
    - Ⓐ feed people
    - Ⓑ feed livestock
    - Ⓒ make ethanol
    - Ⓓ make high fructose corn syrup

11. Coniferous forests cover most of ____.
    - Ⓐ Mexico
    - Ⓑ Canada
    - Ⓒ the United States
    - Ⓓ Panama

12. Where in North America does the Gila monster live?
    - Ⓐ in the desert
    - Ⓑ in the rainforest
    - Ⓒ on the plains
    - Ⓓ in the mountains

13. Which of these is *not* a North American artist?
    - Ⓐ Georgia O'Keeffe
    - Ⓑ Wayne Gretzky
    - Ⓒ Andy Warhol
    - Ⓓ Frida Kahlo

14. The main religion in Mexico is ____.
    - Ⓐ Protestantism
    - Ⓑ Judaism
    - Ⓒ Catholicism
    - Ⓓ Mormonism

15. Which of these groups of people came to Ellis Island between 1892 and 1954?
    - Ⓐ artists
    - Ⓑ soldiers
    - Ⓒ criminals
    - Ⓓ immigrants

16. What do people in Haiti eat to celebrate Independence Day?
    - Ⓐ corn
    - Ⓑ bananas
    - Ⓒ soup
    - Ⓓ candy

SECTION 7

Note Takers

This section provides four note-taker forms that give students the opportunity to culminate their study of North America by doing independent research on places or animals of their choice. (Some suggested topics are given below.) Students may use printed reference materials or Internet sites to gather information on their topics. A cover page is also provided so that students may create a booklet of note takers and any other reproducible pages from the book that you would like students to save.

FORMS

Name ____________________

Physical Feature

Select a physical feature of North America. Write notes about it to complete each section.

____
(Name of Physical Feature)

N W E S

Location

Interesting Facts

Description

Animals or Plants

Name ______________________

Draw a North American animal. Write notes about it to complete each section.

____
(Name of Animal)

Habitat

____
____
____
____

Endangered? Yes No

Physical Characteristics

____
____
____
____

Diet

____
____
____
____

Behaviors

____
____
____
____

Enemies/Defenses

____
____
____
____

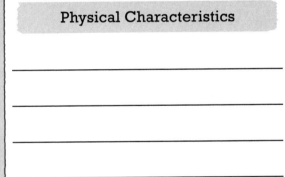

Name ____________________

Tourist Attraction

Draw a North American tourist attraction. Write notes about it to complete each section.

____
(Name of Tourist Attraction)

N
W E
S

Location

____
____
____
____

Interesting Facts

____
____
____
____

Description

____
____
____
____
____
____
____
____
____
____
____

Name ____________________

Select a North American city you'd like to visit. Write notes about it to complete each section.

My Trip to ____________________

(Name of City)

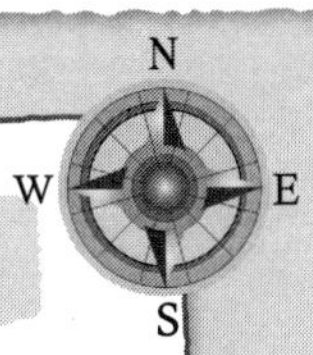

Location

____

____

____

____

How I Would Get There

____

____

____

____

Things I Would See and Do

____

____

____

____

____

____

____

____

____

____

Foods I Would Eat

____

____

____

____

Learning the Language

How to Say "Hello"

____

How to Say "Goodbye"

____

NORTH AMERICA

Page 5

1. B 2. B 3. A 4. C 5. D

Page 6

A. Europe, south, Arctic, east, Pacific

B. Students should color South America orange and Greenland green. They should also circle the Atlantic Ocean with blue, and lower Central America (Panama) with yellow. Finally, they should draw a lion on Africa.

Page 9

A. 1. c	4. e	7. g
2. f	5. d	8. i
3. h	6. b	9. a

B.

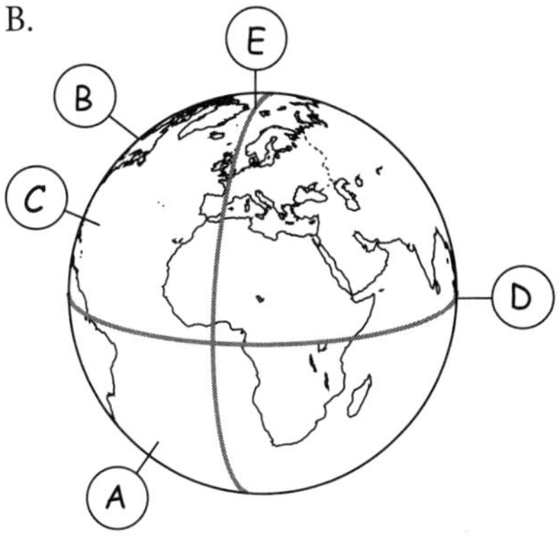

Page 11

A. 1. equator	4. 90°N	7. parallels
2. prime meridian	5. latitude lines	8. 40°N
3. 100°W	6. 15 degrees	9. 150°W

B. because North America is in the Northern and Western hemispheres

Page 12

1. No	6. No
2. Yes	7. No
3. No	8. Yes
4. No	9. Yes
5. Yes	10. Yes

Page 14

Across	Down
2. projection	1. Atlantic
3. Pacific	4. relative
5. hemisphere	6. equator
7. third	
8. Europe	

Page 17

1. B 2. C 3. A 4. B 5. D

Page 18

A. Questions and answers will vary—e.g.,
1. What was the population in 1950? About 220 million.
2. How much did the population increase from 1990 to 2010? It increased by about 110 million.

Page 19

B. 1. tripled	5. 500
2. 2050	6. 649
3. steady	7. two
4. 220	8. 2050

Page 21

Students should color Canada and Greenland green, the seven countries of Central America orange, the islands of the Caribbean yellow, Mexico red, and the United States blue.

Page 22

A. Answers will vary—e.g.,
1. The U.S. is four-and-a-half times larger than Mexico, Honduras, and Nicaragua combined.
2. Canada is the largest country in North America.
3. The U.S. is about five times larger than Mexico.

Page 23

Students should color Canada, the United States, Mexico, Nicaragua, and Honduras each in a different color.

1. Canada	4. Nicaragua
2. United States	5. Honduras
3. Mexico	

Page 24

A. 1. f	6. j
2. g	7. e
3. a	8. i
4. h	9. b
5. c	10. d

B. 1. 2
2. 5

Page 25

C. Answers will vary—e.g.,
1. More people live in the U.S. than all of the other nine most populated countries in North America combined.
2. Cuba is the most populated island in North America.
3. Nicaragua is the tenth most populated country in North America.

Page 26

A.
1. No
2. Yes
3. Yes
4. No
5. No
6. Yes
7. No
8. No
9. Yes
10. Yes

Page 27

B. Answers will vary—e.g.,
1. Yukon Territory shares a border with Alaska.
2. Hudson Bay is surrounded by the provinces of Quebec, Ontario, Manitoba, and Nunavut.
3. Canada is not densely populated.

Page 28

A. regions, capital, Southeast, Hawaii, Alaska, Pacific, territories, Virgin Islands

B. Students should color each of the six regions of the United States a different color and color the map key to match.

C.
1. Rocky Mountain
2. Pacific
3. Northeast and North-Central
4. Northeast and Southeast

Page 30

A. Answers will vary—e.g., New York City has more inhabitants than the combined populations of Philadelphia, Phoenix, San Diego, Dallas, San Antonio, and Detroit.

Page 31

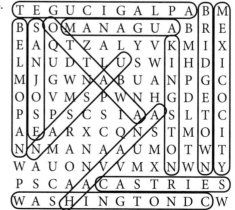

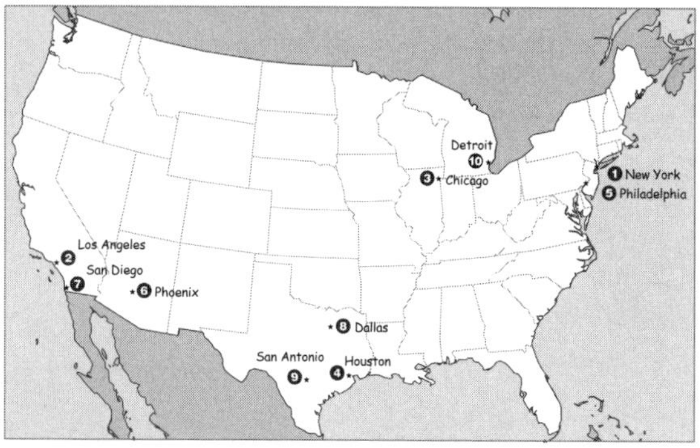

Page 32

A. North America, world, 31, Mexico City

B.
1. Jalisco
2. northwest
3. Baja California Sur
4. Coahuila

Page 33

C. Answers will vary—e.g., The Mexican states of Baja California Norte, Sonora, Chihuahua, Coahuila, Nuevo León, and Tamaulipas border the United States.

Page 34

A.

	Population	**Area**
1.	Guatemala	Nicaragua
2.	Honduras	Honduras
3.	El Salvador	Guatemala
4.	Nicaragua	Panama
5.	Costa Rica	Costa Rica
6.	Panama	Belize
7.	Belize	El Salvador

Page 35

B. Students should color the seven Central American countries different colors and complete the caption. Answers will vary—e.g., El Salvador is the smallest country in terms of area, but it is the third-largest country in terms of population.

C. Answers will vary—e.g.,
1. Belize is the only country that doesn't have access to the Pacific Ocean.
2. El Salvador is the smallest country by area.

Page 36

A.
1. Yes
2. Yes
3. No
4. No
5. Yes
6. Yes
7. No
8. Yes
9. No
10. No

Page 37

B. Students should color Cuba, Jamaica, Haiti, the Dominican Republic, and Puerto Rico. Then they should complete the caption. Answers will vary—e.g., The Lesser Antilles are both the southern- and easternmost islands of the Caribbean.

Page 39

A.
- Costa Rica: San José
- Barbados: Bridgetown
- Canada: Ottawa
- Belize: Belmopan
- Cuba: Havana
- Bahamas: Nassau
- United States: Washington, D.C.
- Mexico: Mexico City
- St. Lucia: Castries
- Nicaragua: Managua
- Jamaica: Kingston
- Honduras: Tegucigalpa

B.

T	E	G	U	C	I	G	A	L	P	A	B	M
B	S	O	M	A	N	A	G	U	A	B	R	E
E	A	Q	T	Z	A	L	Y	V	K	M	I	X
L	N	U	D	T	L	U	S	W	I	H	D	I
M	J	G	W	N	A	B	U	A	N	P	G	C
O	O	V	M	S	P	W	N	H	G	D	E	O
P	S	P	S	C	S	I	A	A	S	L	T	C
A	E	A	R	X	C	Q	N	S	T	M	O	I
N	N	M	A	N	A	A	U	M	O	T	W	T
W	A	U	O	N	V	V	M	X	N	W	N	Y
P	S	C	A	A	C	A	S	T	R	I	E	S
W	A	S	H	I	N	G	T	O	N	D	C	W

Page 40

Across
2. Canada
7. twenty-three
8. population

Down
1. capital
2. Caribbean
3. continental
4. continent
5. seven
6. New York

Page 43

1. B 2. D 3. C 4. B 5. A

Page 44

A. 1. coast ranges
2. Sierra Madre ranges
3. Denali
4. Great Plains
5. Baffin Island
6. Great Basin
7. Canadian Shield
8. Yucatán Peninsula

B. Students should color the following:
Yellow: Chihuahuan Desert, Great Basin Desert, Mojave Desert, Sonoran Desert
Brown: Appalachian Mountains, Coast Ranges, Rocky Mountains, Sierra Madre Ranges
Circled in light green: Coastal Plain, Great Plains
Circled in dark green: Canadian Shield

Page 47

1. Yes
2. No
3. Yes
4. No
5. No
6. No
7. Yes
8. Yes
9. No
10. Yes

B.

Rank	Mountain Peak	Rank	Mountain Peak
1	Mt. Elbert	6	Uncompahgre Peak
2	Mt. Massive	7	Crestone Peak
3	Mt. Harvard	8	Mt. Lincoln
4	La Plata Peak	9	Grays Peak
5	Blanca Peak	10	Mt. Antero

Page 49

A. 1. Arizona
2. 277 miles (446 km)
3. 1 mile (1.6 km)
4. sandstone, shale, limestone
5. Over millions of years, the Colorado River eroded layers of rock.

B. 1. Answers will vary—e.g., I will ride a donkey because I think it will be the most fun.
2. Answers will vary—e.g., hiking boots, snacks, water, sunscreen
3. Answers will vary—e.g., I would like to see different kinds of birds. I would also like to go rafting on the Colorado River.

Page 51

1. southwest
2. a plant
3. pocket mouse
4. Great Basin
5. Mojave
6. Mojave
7. Sonoran
8. Chihuahuan
9. Great Basin
10. Sonoran

Page 52

A. 1. an environment in which the ground is permanently frozen and no trees can grow
2. an area of land that has coniferous forests; cold, snowy winters; and short, warm summers
3. because it has a harsh climate and is mostly covered in ice

Page 53

B. Students should color the taiga green, the tundra purple, and the ice sheet gray. They should also trace the Arctic Circle in red.

Page 54

A. Answers will vary—e.g.,
1. logged for timber
2. cleared to grow crops
3. cleared to create pastures
4. cleared for road construction

Page 55

B. 1. destroyed
2. percent
3. timber
4. pasture
5. kinds
6. government

Crack the Code: spider monkeys

Page 57

1. volcanoes
2. crust
3. North American
4. Montserrat
5. six
6. Grenada
7. 1766

Page 58

A.

Page 58 *(continued)*

B. 1. Chukchi Bay
2. Gulf of California
3. Atlantic Ocean
4. Gulf of Alaska
5. Baffin Bay

Page 60

A. Answers will vary—e.g., Lake Superior, the largest of the Great Lakes, is more than four times bigger than Lake Ontario, the smallest lake.

Page 61

B. 1. Lake Superior
2. Lake Erie
3. Lake Ontario
4. Lake Huron
5. Lake Michigan
6. Lake Superior
7. Lake Ontario
8. Lake Michigan

Page 62

A.

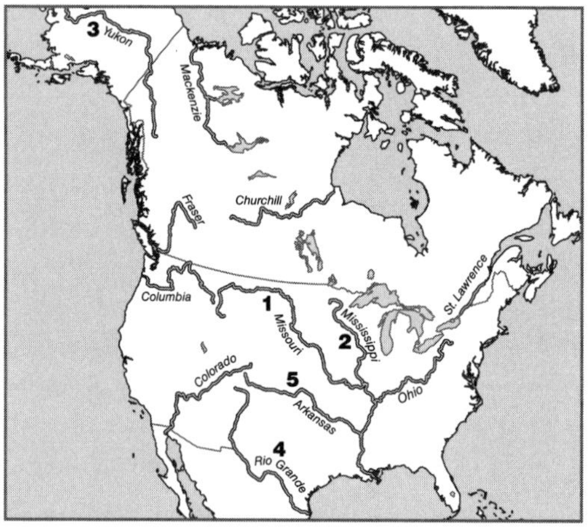

Page 63

B.

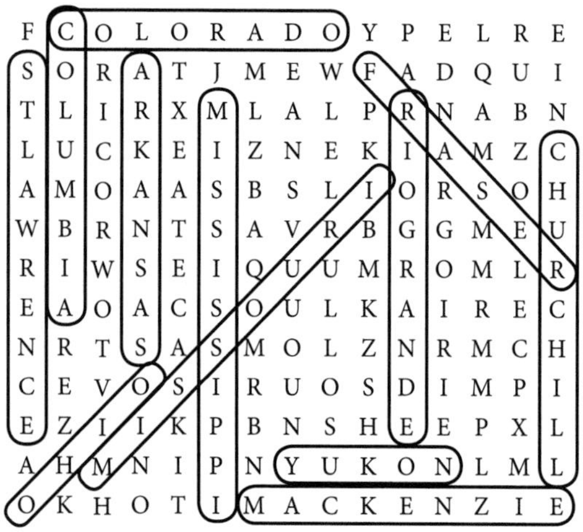

Page 65

1. Atlantic
2. wide
3. eleven
4. locks
5. hinges
6. France
7. August
8. Ancon

Page 66

Across

2. Panama Canal
4. erosion
5. Missouri
7. Gulf of Mexico
8. volcanic

Down

1. Lake Superior
3. rainforest
6. tundra

Page 69

1. C 2. B 3. A 4. B 5. D

Page 71

A. 1. Yes
2. No
3. No
4. Yes
5. No
6. Yes
7. Yes
8. No
9. Yes
10. Yes

B. 1. Mining coal can be harmful to the environment.
2. Burning coal causes pollution.

C. 1. eastern
2. Arctic and Atlantic

Page 73

A. 3, 7, 6, 5, 1, 4, 2

B. Answers will vary—e.g.,
1. They make it impossible for fish to swim upstream and lay their eggs.
2. They make the water warmer, which is not good for some plants and animals.
3. They cause a buildup of mud and silt, which can clog a river.

C. Answers will vary—e.g.,
1. It is a renewable resource.
2. It is relatively inexpensive to produce.
3. It does not cause much pollution.

Page 75

A.

E	C	O	L	L	E	C	T	B	V	H	T	H	E
N	G	N	M	O	Z	E	T	N	E	K	G	T	L
E	R	X	R	M	W	P	O	A	J	Y	E	U	E
R	S	P	E	C	O	N	V	E	R	T	M	R	C
G	W	I	N	D	F	A	R	M	W	Y	I	B	T
Y	H	R	E	I	M	A	T	A	S	Y	B	I	R
E	S	E	W	U	M	G	T	B	E	A	R	N	I
S	O	L	A	R	P	A	N	E	L	T	U	E	C
R	R	T	B	I	E	M	H	E	R	A	T	O	I
N	O	H	L	H	E	S	U	O	Y	O	D	H	T
D	Q	G	E	N	E	R	A	T	O	R	U	E	Y
E	G	E	H	T	E	T	U	C	O	S	Y	A	S

B. Answers will vary—e.g.,

1. In order to catch the greatest amount of wind, wind farms are built in very windy places.
2. Solar panels are used to collect sunlight and change it into electricity.
3. Solar power and wind power are both renewable sources of energy.

Page 77

A. Answers will vary.

B. 1. North Atlantic Ocean
2. Canada
3. pollution, dams, and overfishing
4. They can spread diseases and parasites, and breed with the wild population so their offspring have less of a chance of surviving.

Page 79

1. half
2. corn
3. ethanol
4. feedlots
5. California
6. turkeys

Crack the Code: Holsteins

Page 80

A. 1. over 5 million tons
2. nearly 800,000 tons

Page 81

B. 1. bananas
2. highlands
3. Costa Rica
4. Guatemala
5. bananas
6. coffee

C.

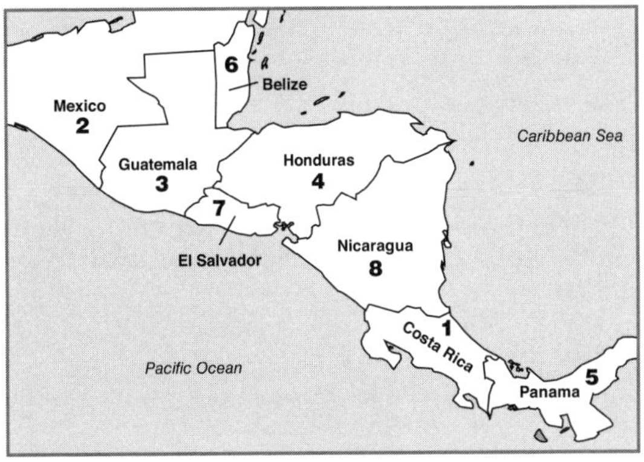

Page 83

1. oxygen
2. needles
3. autumn
4. coniferous
5. medicines
6. New England

Page 87

A. 1. Gila monsters
2. polar bear
3. beaver
4. Gila monster
5. humpback whale
6. polar bear
7. Quetzals
8. humpback whale
9. Bison
10. Beavers

B. Answers will vary.

Page 88

Across
1. corn
2. renewable
5. quetzals
7. salmon

Down
1. coniferous
3. bananas
4. fossil
6. bison

Page 91

1. B 2. D 3. D 4. A 5. C

Page 93

A. 1. Ellis Island
2. immigrants
3. Monument
4. Mexico
5. Mayans
6. pyramid
7. steps
8. court
9. Citadel
10. turrets

B. Answers will vary—e.g., I would like to visit Ellis Island because it is a big part of America's history.

Page 94

1. f 2. c 3. a 4. g 5. b 6. d 7. e

Page 95

Answers will vary.

Page 96

1. No 2. Yes 3. No 4. No 5. Yes

Page 97

Same: They both wrote stories based on their own personal experiences and both were teachers.

Different: Wilder grew up in a family that traveled through the Midwest, while Angelou was raised in the South. Angelou dealt with segregation, while Wilder did not.

Page 99

1. Stanley Cup
2. Hoboken
3. Edmonton
4. Mexico
5. Super Bowl
6. Canada
7. World Cup

Crack the Code: New York Yankees

Page 100

1. Lutheran
2. Catholic
3. Spanish
4. Ireland
5. Baptists
6. Mormon
7. Amish

Page 101

1. Islam, Judaism, Buddhism, Hinduism
2. Toronto and Montreal
3. There are more Muslim immigrants. Some North American citizens are converting to Islam.

Page 103

Answers will vary—e.g.,

Inuit:
1. Their diet consisted mainly of meat.
2. They used dogs to pull sleds over snow.

Cherokee:
1. They developed their own system of governing, modeled after the American government.
2. Cherokee villages were usually built near a river.

Tarahumara:
1. Most still live a traditional lifestyle, without modern technology.
2. They hunt by chasing an animal until it gets too tired to run anymore.

Page 105

A.

A	B	T	Y	K	H	S	G	T	I	P	A	J	M
D	F	S	V	A	E	B	X	O	G	E	U	O	P
C	P	C	L	E	U	G	N	S	G	L	B	U	D
D	B	H	C	Z	C	H	I	T	H	A	A	E	E
G	E	I	G	A	M	L	S	A	B	U	E	N	I
Z	R	L	C	O	C	A	M	D	E	E	P	C	O
Q	I	I	N	O	S	H	A	A	P	A	O	H	R
U	W	E	E	L	T	R	E	X	P	G	V	I	E
B	K	S	A	E	I	C	Q	L	N	M	E	L	T
S	N	S	E	B	T	O	P	A	P	A	Y	A	I
R	A	P	D	Z	N	N	M	A	A	E	V	D	T
Y	C	T	H	R	E	C	W	T	A	S	J	A	U
J	P	O	A	I	N	H	B	E	A	N	S	V	K
W	O	C	R	C	A	B	A	N	A	N	A	T	L
A	M	S	E	N	R	Z	L	P	O	W	O	T	Y

B. Answers will vary.

Page 106

1. France
2. September 15
3. a special parade to celebrate the Bahamas' independence from Great Britain
4. because in the past, French colonists did not allow them to eat soup

Page 107

Mexico, November, cemeteries, picnics, shrines, skeletons, Pan de Muertos

Page 108

Across	Down
2. photographer	1. reggae
4. immigrants	3. Haiti
7. Mexico	5. Mormon
8. pelau	6. Stanley

Page 110

1. Rocky Mountains
2. Canada
3. Missouri River
4. New York City
5. Mojave Desert
6. Pacific Ocean
7. Atlantic Ocean
8. Mexico
9. Honduras
10. Caribbean Islands

Page 111

1. B 2. A 3. D 4. A 5. A 6. C 7. C 8. B

Page 112

9. C 10. B 11. B 12. A 13. B 14. C 15. D 16. C

Sampler

Daily Geography Practice
Grade 5 • Week 31

WEEK 31

Daily Geography

Skill: Cooperative Solutions
Essential Element 4: Standard 13

Time Zones of the United States

Introducing the Map

Ask students what it would be like if every community in the United States used a different time. The obvious answer is that people would be confused and many problems would be created. To avoid this confusion, a cooperative system was designed called *standard time zones*. Talk about the advantages of having regional time zones.

Explain the concept of time zones. A day is 24 hours long—the time it takes Earth to complete one rotation on its axis. Earth is divided into 24 time zones. The United States is divided into six of those twenty-four time zones.

Show students the Time Zones of the United States map. Tell students that each zone uses a time one hour different from its neighboring zones. The hours are earlier to the west of each zone and later to the east.

Go over all the names of the time zones and have students notice the one hour difference between each of them. Talk about how Alaska is so large that it covers two time zones. Explain that some of the Aleutian Islands of Alaska are so far west that scientists placed them with Hawaii, thus creating Hawaiian-Aleutian Time.

Ask students which time zone Chicago, Illinois, is in. They will probably say Central Time. Then ask them: If it is 3:00 P.M. in Chicago, what time is it in Denver? The answer is 2:00 P.M. Ask students a couple more questions, each time changing the local times to help students understand the concept.

Extend the lesson to discuss daylight saving time. This is a plan in which clocks are set one hour ahead of standard time for a certain period of time. The plan provides for an additional hour of daylight. It begins on the first Sunday in April and ends on the last Sunday in October. Most states choose to go on daylight saving time, but several don't. Talk about how that complicates things.

Introducing Vocabulary

daylight saving time a plan in which clocks are set one hour ahead of standard time for a specific period of time

standard time zone a region in which the same time is used

time zone a region in which the same time is used; Earth is divided into 24 time zones

ANSWER KEY

Note: Not all questions can be answered with information from the map. Students will have to use their mental map skills to locate places on the map.

Monday

1. 6; Hawaiian-Aleutian, Alaskan, Pacific, Mountain, Central, and Eastern Times
2. one hour

Tuesday

1. earlier
2. Eastern Time

Wednesday

1. Hawaiian-Aleutian Time
2. 11:00 A.M.

Thursday

1. 10:00 P.M.
2. North Dakota, South Dakota, Nebraska, Kansas, and Texas

Friday

1. No, it's 2:00 A.M. and Grandfather is probably sleeping.
2. It is Daylight Saving Time.

Challenge

Answers will vary, but students should make up two questions and provide answers to the questions.

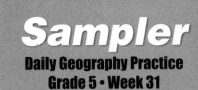

Name

Time Zones of the United States

Daylight Saving Time begins on the first Sunday in April and ends on the last Sunday in October. Remember this trick to set your clocks one hour ahead in the spring and one hour back in the fall: ***Spring ahead*; Fall back.**

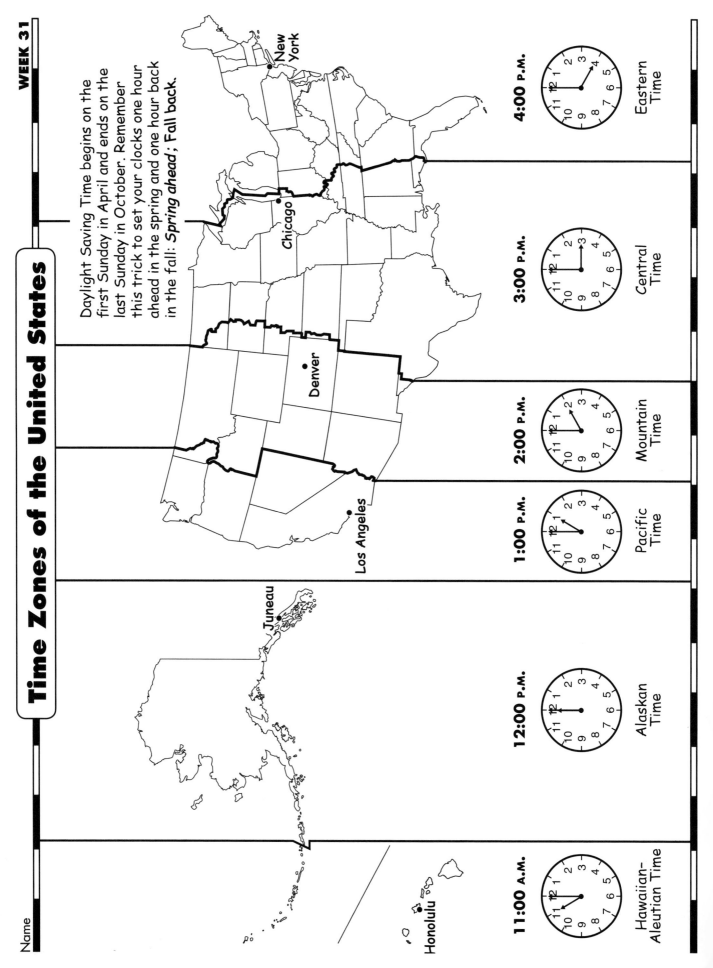

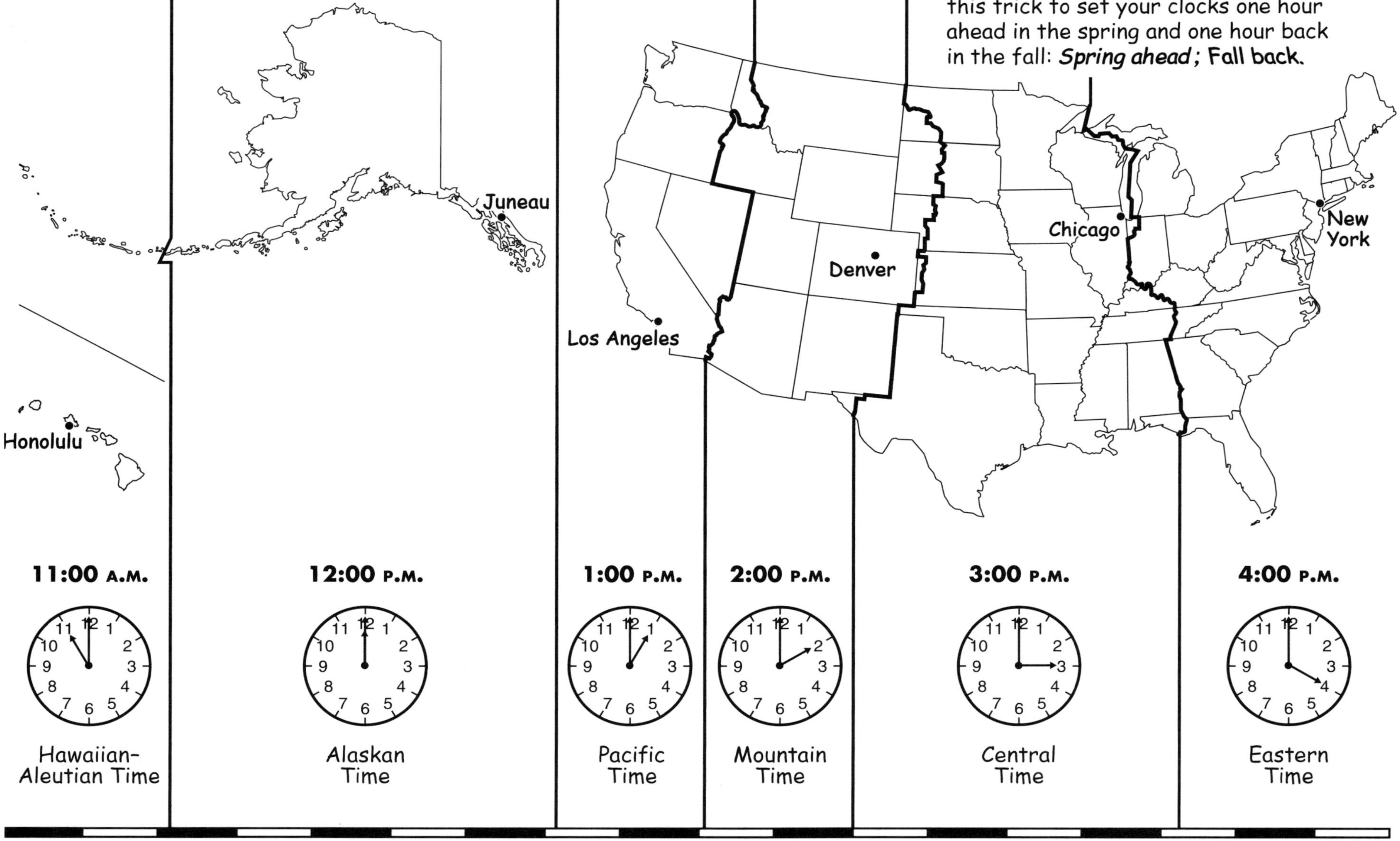

Name ____________________________________

Daily Geography

WEEK 31

Time Zones of the United States

Monday

1. The United States is divided into how many standard time zones? Name them from west to east.

____

____

____

2. What is the time difference between each neighboring time zone?

____

Tuesday

1. Are the hours earlier or later to the west of each time zone?

____

2. Cities in the Northeast region are part of which time zone?

____

Wednesday

1. Which time zone includes Hawaii and some of the western islands of Alaska?

____

2. If it is 1:00 P.M. in Chicago, what time is it in Los Angeles?

____

Name ____________________

Daily Geography

WEEK 31

Time Zones of the United States

Thursday

1. If it is midnight in Chicago, what time is it in Seattle, Washington?

____

2. Which states have areas that are part of Central and Mountain Time Zones?

____

____

____

Friday

1. If you live in Honolulu and it is 9:00 P.M., is it a good time to call your grandfather in New York? Why or why not?

____

____

2. It is the first Sunday in April and clocks have been set one hour ahead. Why?

____

Challenge

Make up two time zone questions. Write your questions on the back of the map. Don't forget to include the answer. Pair up with a classmate and ask each other the time zone questions.